COMPACT CABINS

The mission of Storey Publishing is to serve our customers by
publishing practical information that encourages
personal independence in harmony with the environment.

Edited by Deborah Balmuth and Nancy Ringer
Art direction by Alethea Morrison
Book design and production by McFadden and Thorpe

Illustrations by Steve Sanford
Floor plans by the author
Indexed by Catherine F. Goddard

    The information in this book is true and complete to the best of our knowledge. All recommen-
dations are made without guarantee on the part of the author or Storey Publishing. The author and
publisher disclaim any liability in connection with the use of this information.
    Storey books are available for special premium and promotional uses and for customized edi-
tions. For further information, please call 1-800-793-9396.

Storey Publishing
210 MASS MoCA Way
North Adams, MA 01247
www.storey.com

Printed in the United States by Courier
10 9 8 7 6 5 4 3 2 1

LIBRARY OF CONGRESS CATALOGING-IN-PUBLICATION DATA

Rowan, Gerald.
  Compact cabins / by Gerald Rowan.
    p. cm.
  Includes index.
  ISBN 978-1-60342-462-2 (pbk. : alk. paper)
  1. Log cabins—Design and construction.
  2. Log cabins—Designs and plans. I. Title.
TH4840.R687 2010
728.7'3—dc22
                    2009028677

COMPACT CABINS

Simple Living in 1,000 Square Feet or Less

by Gerald Rowan

Storey Publishing

INTRODUCTION:
GOOD LIVING IN SMALL SPACES

MOST OF US DREAM OF HAVING A SMALL PLACE ON A LAKE, IN THE MOUNTAINS, ON THE SHORE, IN THE WOODS, OR EVEN IN OUR BACKYARD. SOME DREAM OF A PLACE FOR PRIVACY AND SOLITUDE.

Some dream of a place to make art or write. Some dream of a place for fishing, getting out in nature, or simply spending time with friends and family.

One giant impediment to owning a cabin is the cost of building one. An excellent way to control that cost is to build small. In fact, building small offers a number of advantages: lower cost, lower impact on the environment, reduced use of building materials, reduced building time, and less maintenance.

One inherent problem with building small is creating space that is comfortable to live in and meets our needs. Good design can keep the costs and environmental impact to a minimum and still create comfortable living space. And that is the focus of this book. The ideas presented here are intended for folks who want to have a hand in designing their own small cabin in order to create a space that fits their needs in a simpler, more affordable, more ecological way.

Some folks object to the idea of living in a small space, and they have a point: a cramped, crowded space would make anyone feel a bit claustrophobic. But in a well-designed space, small does not mean cramped. Good design imbues even a small space with ample light and ventilation, enough room for people to move about easily, comfortable furnishings, and all the amenities that home dwellers require to enjoy cabin life.

The fifty cabin plans in chapter 1 run the gamut from just more than 150 square feet to just under 1,000 square feet. Each cabin's design makes the most of its size to offer comfortable living, working, and sleeping quarters — in short, good living in a small space.

Each design is detailed as a floor plan and an elevation, and you should feel free to mix and match floor plans and elevations. As a general rule, floor plans are about ergonomics, or people space. Elevations are generally about design or style. Any cabin floor plan may have a dozen different elevations and rooflines that would work with it, just as any elevation may have a large number of floor plans that would work well with it. Each will impart a very different sense of style.

Many of the cabin designs contain elements that can be selectively applied to other designs. For example, the outdoor freestanding fireplace designed for one cabin's porch would work equally well on another design's porch. The out-door storage locker of one cabin could easily be converted to the nerve center of a solar-electric system for another off-the-grid cabin.

Design doesn't end with a floor plan and elevation. The remaining chapters address the elements of the plans you'll see in chapter 1, from off-the-grid power systems to appliance choices, premanufactured structural components, ecological building choices, and space-saving (or space-enhancing) design features. All these cabin elements play a role in the design of a cabin that works best for you.

Designing a cabin as a series of modules can greatly facilitate the building process, and it makes future expansion simple. Chapter 3 discusses the modular concept in more detail. There you'll find modules for kitchens, baths, living spaces, bedrooms, porches and decks, and combinations of all of these. Such modules can be strung together to produce a variety of cabin sizes and layouts. A modular plan allows you to build a starter module and live in it as you construct the rest of the cabin.

Though this book offers many design ideas and plans, if you are not a builder or architect, you will need to work with one to create a detailed building plan. You will also need to consult with your local building department to make sure that your plans conform to local building and zoning codes.

Some people dream of the ultimate cabin, one that has every comfort; some dream of a minimalist cabin deep in the woods. Most of us dream somewhere in between. Whatever your dream, know that you *can* live well in a small space. I hope this book will help you get there.

50 DESIGNS FOR COMPACT CABINS

YOU'LL FIND HERE FIFTY INNOVATIVE CABIN DESIGNS TO SUIT ANY SITE, BUDGET, OR LIFESTYLE, ALL IN LESS THAN 1,000 SQUARE FEET.

Compact Definitions

In designs that follow, the term **micro** refers to cabins that are less than 300 square feet. The term **mini** refers to cabins that are between 300 and 500 square feet. All the rest are considered simply **compact**.

They are arranged by size, from the smallest to the largest, with the square footage determined by enclosed space (not including, for example, open porches or decks). Some are named after state parks and natural features in my native Poconos region, while others have more prosaic names based on their notable features. Each cabin is complete unto itself, but the features of any cabin could be combined with the features of others to create new designs.

Each design notes the number of people it will sleep and the size of the kitchen and bathroom.

➻ **Kitchens:** A *full* kitchen contains a four-burner range, a 10- to 14-cubic-foot refrigerator, and a sink. A *three-quarter* kitchen contains a two- or three-burner range, an 8- to 10-cubic-foot refrigerator, and a sink. A *half* kitchen contains a two-burner range, a 3- to 8-cubic-foot refrigerator, and a sink.

➻ **Bathrooms:** A *full* bathroom contains a shower over a tub, a full-sized toilet, and a sink. A *three-quarter* bathroom contains a shower, a toilet, and a sink. A *half* bath contains a toilet and a shower and shares a sink with the kitchen.

Sleeping accommodations are listed as full-sized bed, Murphy bed, daybed, bunk bed, single bed, pullout sofa, or folding dinette.

The floor plans are to the scale of $\frac{1}{8}$ inch = 1 foot. With the use of an architect's scale (available at drafting or art supply stores), you can take measurements from them in order to incorporate ideas into your own designs.

MICRO CABIN

This tiny cabin is based on ideas gleaned from the travel trailer industry to utilize space very efficiently. In a cabin this small, electric space heat makes sense.

Features
162 square feet
Half kitchen
Half bath
Sleeps 2
Utilizes RV components
Adaptable to being off the grid

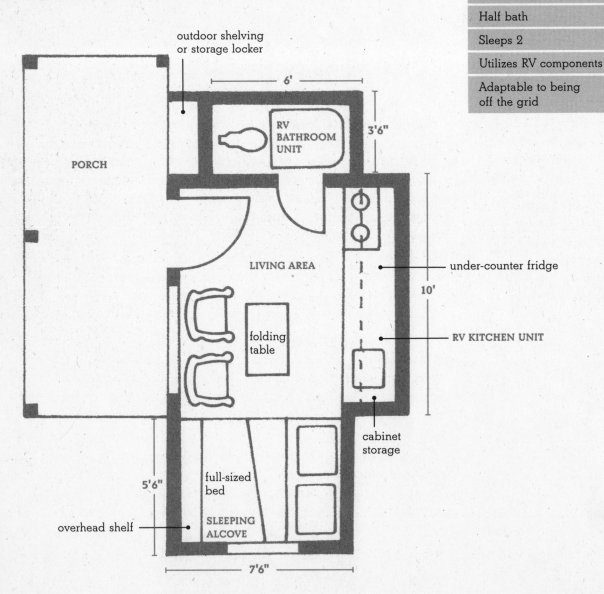

COVERED PORCH: could be enclosed as additional living space.

PITCHED ROOF: could support solar panels if oriented to the south.

OUTSIDE STORAGE LOCKER: is ideal for storing fishing gear or housing batteries for a solar-electric system.

SLEEPING ALCOVE: provides storage with an overhead shelf and under-bed drawers or boxes.

PERSONAL CABIN

This cabin is just the right size for a personal retreat. With the addition of bunkbeds it becomes a getaway for two. This design calls for a small woodstove; if you intend to use the cabin as only a three-season retreat, an electric space heater would work well.

DAYBED: doubles as a couch and a bed; if replaced with a bunk bed, this cabin could easily accommodate two people.

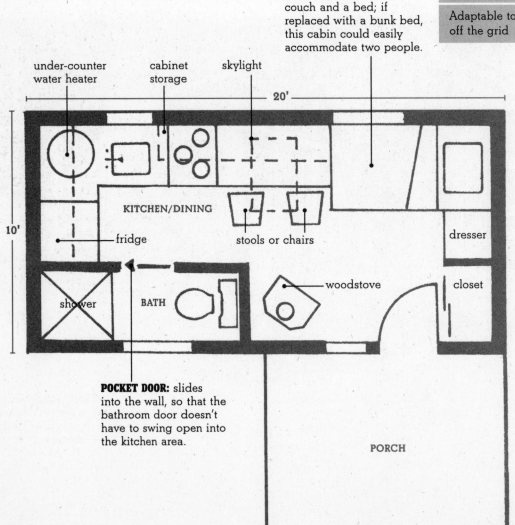

under-counter water heater

cabinet storage

skylight

20'

10'

KITCHEN/DINING

fridge

stools or chairs

dresser

woodstove

closet

shower

BATH

POCKET DOOR: slides into the wall, so that the bathroom door doesn't have to swing open into the kitchen area.

PORCH

GABLE WINDOWS: let in light from each end of the cabin.

OPERABLE SKYLIGHT: on back side of roof can be opened for natural ventilation.

PITCHED ROOF: could support solar panels if oriented to the south.

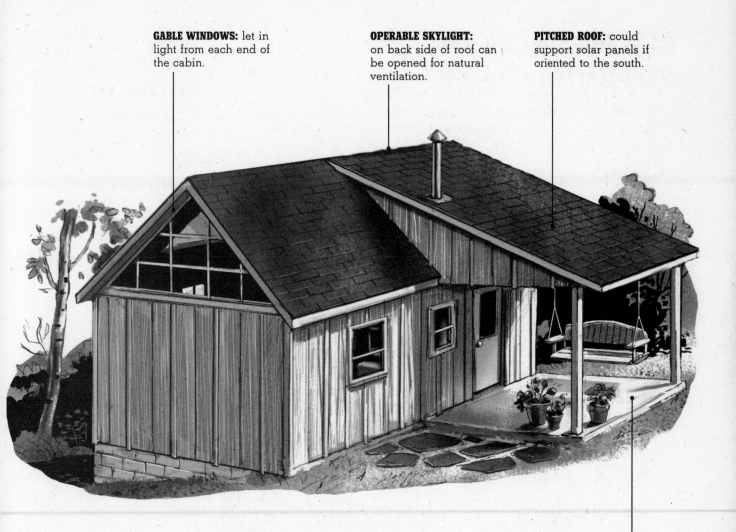

PORCH: can be altered to become a deck or enclosed as additional living space.

MICRO CABIN WITH OUTDOOR CLOSET

A roomy outdoor closet can be useful if you have a lot of fishing, hunting, boating, or other gear to store. It also can house a sizable battery array for a solar-electric system.

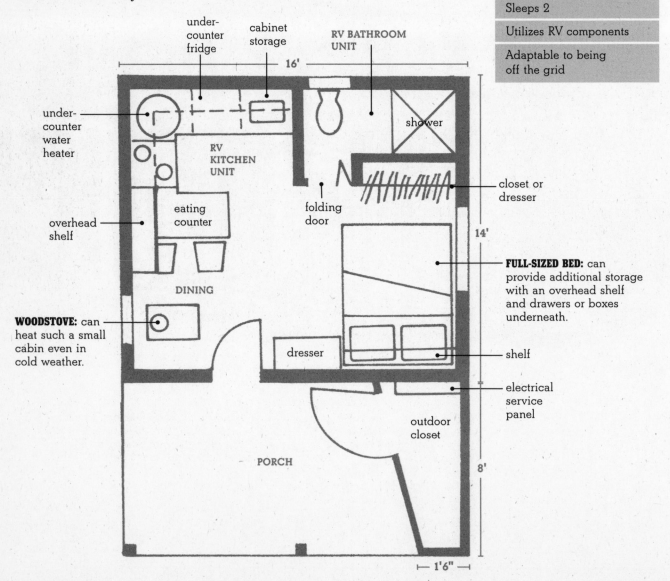

under- counter fridge

cabinet storage

RV BATHROOM UNIT

16'

under- counter water heater

RV KITCHEN UNIT

shower

eating counter

overhead shelf

folding door

closet or dresser

14'

DINING

FULL-SIZED BED: can provide additional storage with an overhead shelf and drawers or boxes underneath.

WOODSTOVE: can heat such a small cabin even in cold weather.

dresser

shelf

electrical service panel

outdoor closet

PORCH

8'

1'6"

PITCHED ROOF: could support solar panels if oriented to the south.

CLERESTORY WINDOWS: bring light to the interior and could be opened in warm weather for natural ventilation.

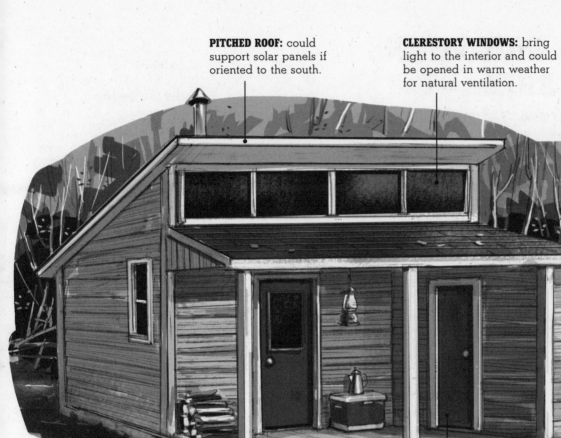

PORCH: can begin life as a deck, then be screened in and eventually framed in with operable windows.

OUTSIDE CLOSET: is ideal for storing bulky gear and to house batteries for a solar-electric system.

ENDLESS MOUNTAINS MICRO CABIN

This cabin is a perfect getaway for two, and when the couch is pulled out, it can sleep an additional two guests. For a cabin this small the heating options are many: the design calls for gas-fired space heating, but electric space heating, a hot water circulation system (see page 196), or a small woodstove would also work well.

Features
250 square feet
Half kitchen
Three-quarter bath
Sleeps 2 to 4
Adaptable to being off the grid

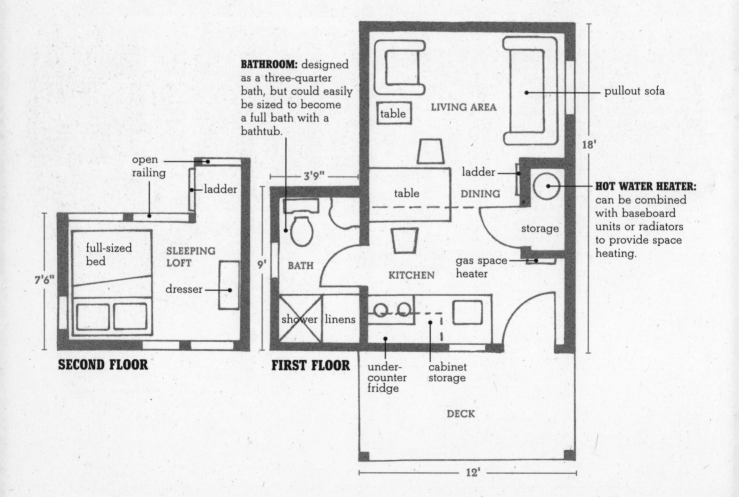

BATHROOM: designed as a three-quarter bath, but could easily be sized to become a full bath with a bathtub.

open railing

ladder

SLEEPING LOFT

full-sized bed

dresser

7'6"

SECOND FLOOR

3'9"

9'

BATH

shower   linens

FIRST FLOOR

under-counter fridge

cabinet storage

table

table

LIVING AREA

ladder

DINING

KITCHEN

storage

gas space heater

DECK

12'

18'

pullout sofa

HOT WATER HEATER: can be combined with baseboard units or radiators to provide space heating.

PITCHED ROOF: could support solar panels if oriented to the south.

DECK: can be any size; should be designed to maximize the view from the front of the cabin.

MICRO CLERESTORY CABIN

At just 256 square feet, this cabin has some surprising amenities, including a full kitchen and bath. The bank of clerestory windows allows light into the center and also provides natural ventilation.

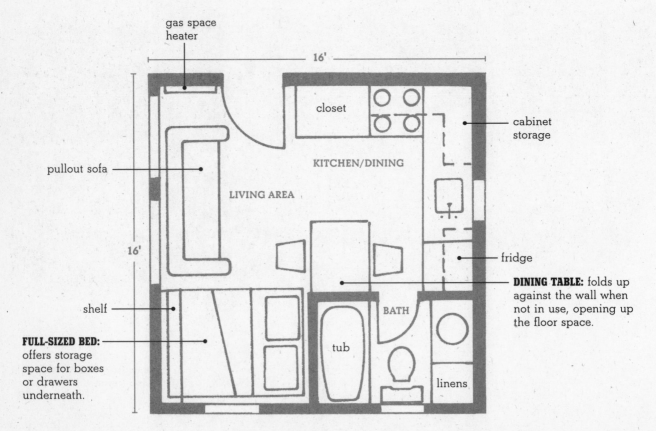

gas space heater

16'

closet

cabinet storage

KITCHEN/DINING

pullout sofa

LIVING AREA

16'

fridge

DINING TABLE: folds up against the wall when not in use, opening up the floor space.

shelf

BATH

FULL-SIZED BED: offers storage space for boxes or drawers underneath.

tub

linens

CLERESTORY WINDOWS: bring light to the interior and can be opened in warm weather for natural ventilation.

PITCHED ROOF: could support solar panels if oriented to the south.

HIGH KNOB CABIN

A cabin with all the traditional amenities. The fireplace provides heat and the romance of a roaring fire on cold evenings.

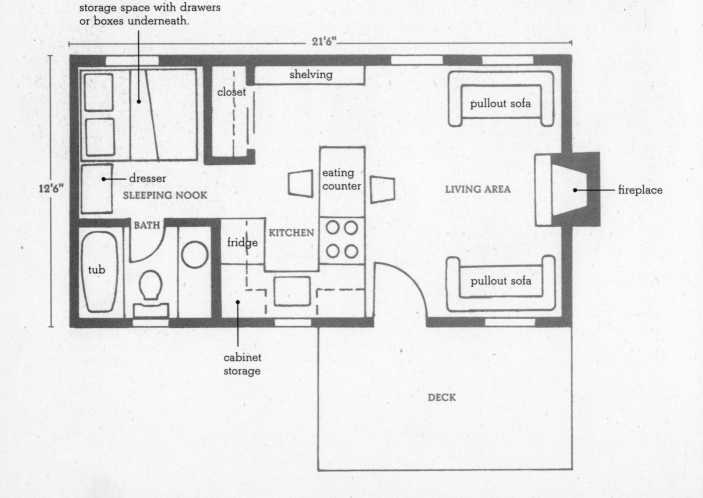

FULL-SIZED BED: offers storage space with drawers or boxes underneath.

21'6"

12'6"

closet

shelving

dresser

SLEEPING NOOK

eating counter

pullout sofa

LIVING AREA

fireplace

BATH

fridge

KITCHEN

tub

cabinet storage

pullout sofa

DECK

UPPER-LEVEL WINDOWS: bring light to the interior of the cabin, helping it feel open and cheery.

PITCHED ROOF: could support solar panels if oriented to the south.

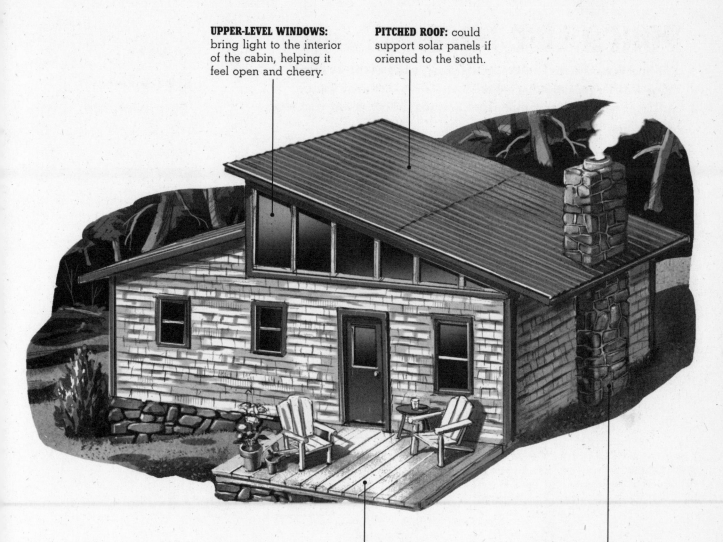

DECK: could be converted to a porch or framed in as additional living space.

FIELDSTONE FIREPLACE: acts as a heat sink, retaining heat and then releasing it back into the living space. This process could be enhanced by bringing the fireplace entirely inside as a Russian stove.

PORCH LIFE MICRO CABIN

A perfect getaway. The enclosed porch functions as a three-season room, with large banks of windows that, if oriented to the south, can act as passive solar components, keeping the porch warm enough to enjoy in cold weather.

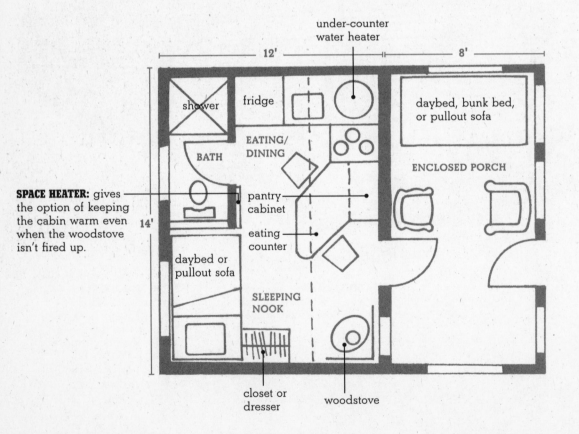

under-counter water heater

12'

8'

shower

fridge

daybed, bunk bed, or pullout sofa

EATING/ DINING

BATH

ENCLOSED PORCH

SPACE HEATER: gives the option of keeping the cabin warm even when the woodstove isn't fired up.

14'

pantry cabinet

eating counter

daybed or pullout sofa

SLEEPING NOOK

closet or dresser

woodstove

OVERHEAD STORAGE: is possible in the space over the sleeping area; it could be accessed via a pull-down attic ladder.

PITCHED ROOF: could support solar panels if oriented to the south.

CLERESTORY WINDOWS: bring light to the interior of the cabin, helping it feel open and cheery, and can be opened for natural ventilation.

BAER ROCKS CABIN

This cabin works well in steep building sites, such as along the bank of a stream or river. Its dimensions lend themselves to off-site building; the main unit of the cabin can be trailered in, and the deck built on-site.

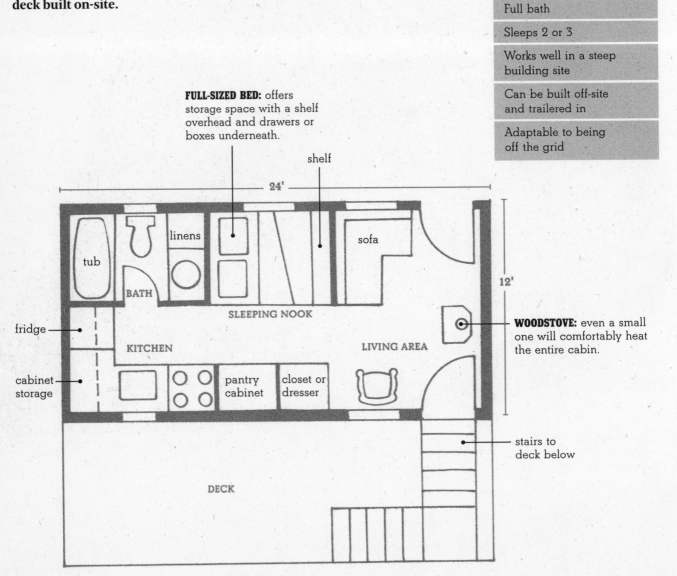

FULL-SIZED BED: offers storage space with a shelf overhead and drawers or boxes underneath.

shelf

24'

12'

tub

linens

sofa

BATH

SLEEPING NOOK

fridge

WOODSTOVE: even a small one will comfortably heat the entire cabin.

KITCHEN

LIVING AREA

cabinet storage

pantry cabinet

closet or dresser

stairs to deck below

DECK

PITCHED ROOF: could accommodate solar panels if oriented to the south.

EXPANSIVE DECK: offers plenty of room for relaxing outdoors, with great views.

CLASSIC SIXTIES A-FRAME

Traditional A-frame cabins have an inherent interior space problem. To overcome that problem, giving the cabin plenty of usable floor space, this design adds a shed dormer on one side and designates the other side for storage.

Features

288 square feet

Full kitchen

Three-quarter bath

Sleeps 2

Adaptable to being off the grid

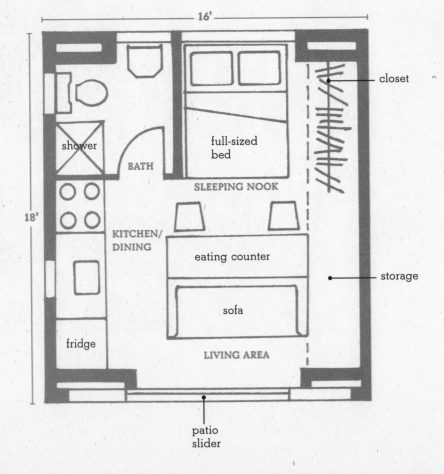

closet

full-sized bed

SLEEPING NOOK

shower

BATH

KITCHEN/ DINING

eating counter

storage

sofa

fridge

LIVING AREA

16'

18'

patio slider

PITCHED ROOF: could support solar panels if oriented to the south.

GLASS END WALL: can provide passive solar heating if positioned to face south.

PATIO SLIDING DOOR: combines with windows to create an all-glass end wall, helping the cabin feel open to the outdoors.

DECK: can easily be added on, increasing the cabin's usable space and easing the transition from indoors to outdoors.

MICRO CABIN WITH LOFT

Based on the 12-foot-square modules described in chapter 2, this cabin is compact but offers all the necessary amenities. The loft, accessed by a ship's ladder, gives some privacy to the sleeping space. Space heating is accomplished through the use of a catalytic gas heater. In a cabin this small, electric space heat would also make sense.

Features
288 square feet
Half kitchen
Half bath
Sleeps 2
Adaptable to being off the grid

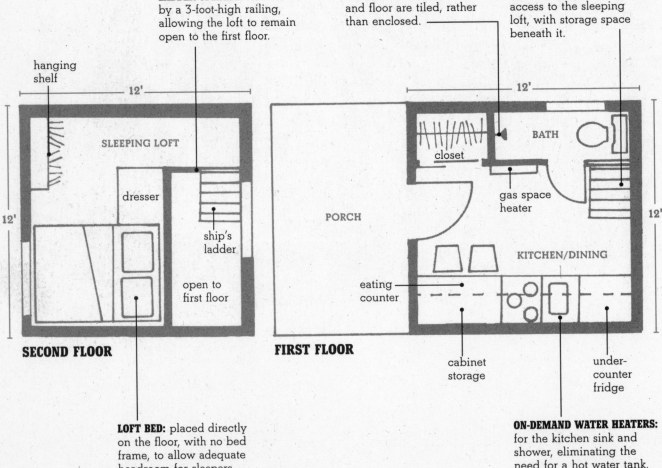

LADDER OPENING: framed by a 3-foot-high railing, allowing the loft to remain open to the first floor.

BATHROOM SHOWER: walls and floor are tiled, rather than enclosed.

SHIP'S LADDER: provides access to the sleeping loft, with storage space beneath it.

hanging shelf

12'

SLEEPING LOFT

12'

dresser

ship's ladder

open to first floor

SECOND FLOOR

12'

closet

BATH

gas space heater

PORCH

eating counter

KITCHEN/DINING

12'

FIRST FLOOR

LOFT BED: placed directly on the floor, with no bed frame, to allow adequate headroom for sleepers.

cabinet storage

under-counter fridge

ON-DEMAND WATER HEATERS: for the kitchen sink and shower, eliminating the need for a hot water tank.

UPPER-LEVEL WINDOWS: provide a view from the sleeping loft and light to the interior of the cabin.

ROOFLINE: pitch and position can be altered to maximize sun exposure for solar panels.

SOLAR-POWERED MICRO CABIN

Designed for an off-the-grid application, this cabin relies on solar power for electricity and water heating. The woodstove provides heat in colder weather.

Features
290 square feet
Half kitchen
Half bath
Sleeps 2 or 3
Designed to be off the grid

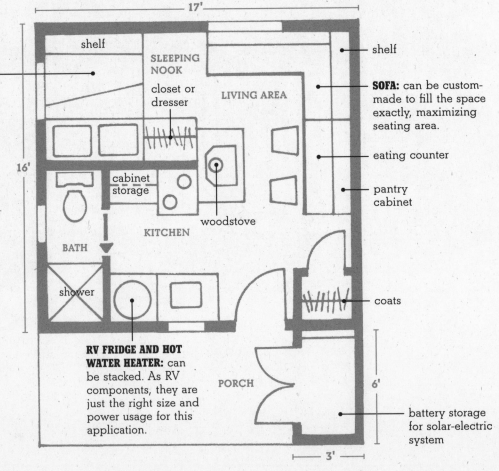

FULL-SIZED BED: offers storage space with a shelf overhead and drawers or boxes underneath.

shelf

SLEEPING NOOK

closet or dresser

LIVING AREA

shelf

SOFA: can be custom-made to fill the space exactly, maximizing seating area.

eating counter

pantry cabinet

cabinet storage

woodstove

KITCHEN

BATH

shower

coats

RV FRIDGE AND HOT WATER HEATER: can be stacked. As RV components, they are just the right size and power usage for this application.

PORCH

battery storage for solar-electric system

17'

16'

6'

3'

PITCHED ROOF: accommodates both solar-electric and solar hot water panels.

PIERS: allow for under-cabin ventilation, helping to keep it cool and dry; a traditional mortar foundation could be substituted in cooler climates.

PORCH: can be open or screened, or could be framed in as additional living space.

MINI CLERESTORY CABIN

The roof design of this cabin accommodates clerestory windows, which allow light deep within the cabin and provide natural ventilation, easing or eliminating the need for air conditioning.

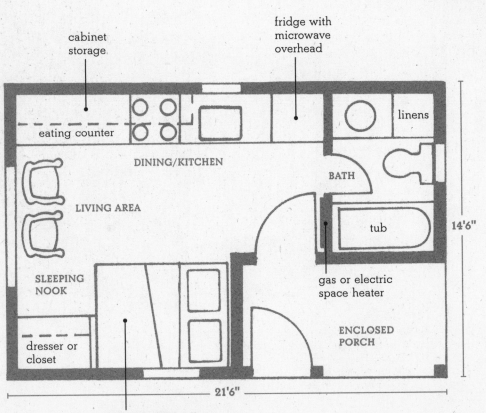

cabinet storage

fridge with microwave overhead

eating counter

linens

DINING/KITCHEN

BATH

LIVING AREA

tub

SLEEPING NOOK

14'6"

gas or electric space heater

ENCLOSED PORCH

dresser or closet

21'6"

FULL-SIZED BED: offers storage space for boxes or drawers underneath.

CLERESTORY WINDOWS: bring light to the interior and can be opened in warm weather for natural ventilation.

PORCH: screened to allow cabin dwellers to enjoy the outdoors without the bugs.

PITCHED ROOF: could support solar panels if oriented to the south.

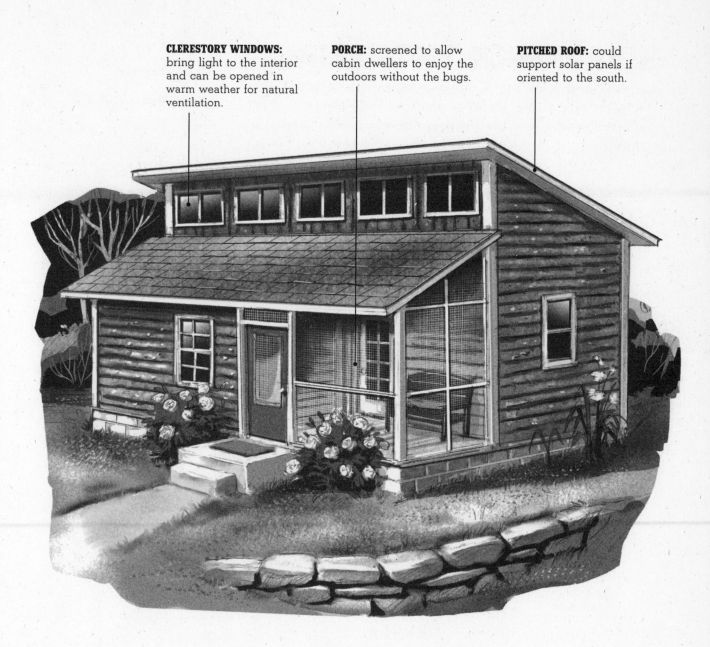

ADIRONDACK TWIG CABIN

Twig cabins are classic Adirondack style. Materials to build this cabin may be gathered on-site; any trees cut to make space for the cabin can be recycled as part of the twig architecture. The cabin's appeal is completely rustic, yet it houses a full modern kitchen and bathroom.

Features
323 square feet
Full kitchen
Full bath
Sleeps 4 to 6
Fireplace

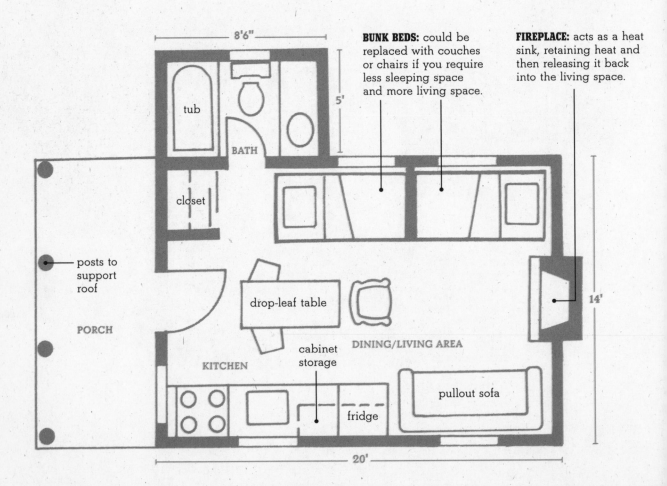

BUNK BEDS: could be replaced with couches or chairs if you require less sleeping space and more living space.

FIREPLACE: acts as a heat sink, retaining heat and then releasing it back into the living space.

8'6"

5'

tub

BATH

closet

posts to support roof

PORCH

drop-leaf table

DINING/LIVING AREA

14'

cabinet storage

KITCHEN

fridge

pullout sofa

20'

TWIG STYLE: uses unmilled branches and logs as posts and beams, bringing a naturalistic character to the cabin architecture.

GREAT OUTDOORS MINI CABIN

If the outdoor life is your thing, this cabin design is an excellent choice. For cooking outdoors, it offers an expansive porch complete with an outside fireplace. And if you make use of all the sleeping options, it sleeps up to seven people.

Features

325 square feet

Three-quarter kitchen

Three-quarter bath

Sleeps 2 to 7

Outdoor fireplace

Adaptable to being off the grid

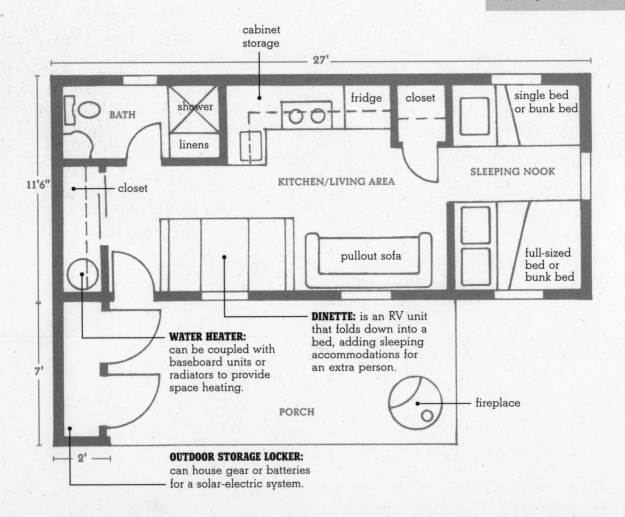

cabinet storage

27'

BATH

shower

linens

fridge

closet

single bed or bunk bed

11'6"

closet

KITCHEN/LIVING AREA

SLEEPING NOOK

pullout sofa

full-sized bed or bunk bed

DINETTE: is an RV unit that folds down into a bed, adding sleeping accommodations for an extra person.

WATER HEATER: can be coupled with baseboard units or radiators to provide space heating.

7'

PORCH

fireplace

2'

OUTDOOR STORAGE LOCKER: can house gear or batteries for a solar-electric system.

PITCHED ROOF: could support solar panels if oriented to the south.

CLERESTORY WINDOWS: bring light to the interior and can be opened in warm weather for natural ventilation.

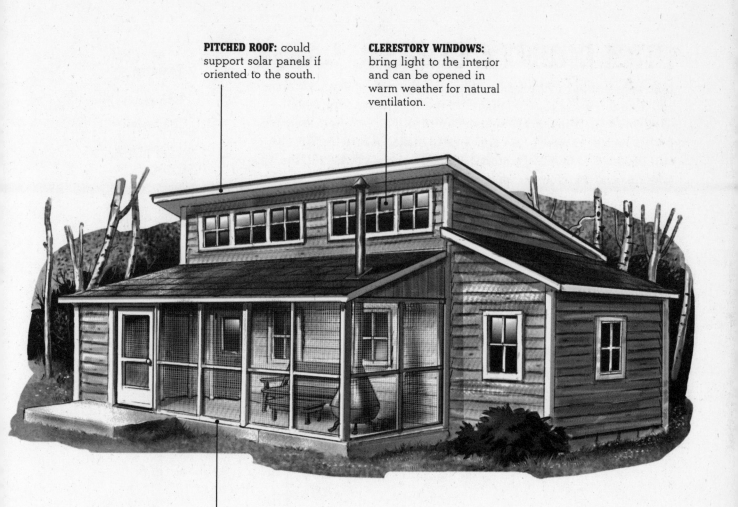

PORCH: can be open or screened, or redesigned as a deck, or framed in as additional living space.

PIKE COUNTY CLASSIC CABIN

Pike County is one of the rockiest places in the state of Pennsylvania, and probably in the country, thanks to the last great glacier, which left behind an abundance of rounded river rock. Cabins here are often built from the very stone that is cleared to make room to build them. Stone is an ideal building material for damp places or where it is readily available and therefore inexpensive.

Features
340 square feet
Full kitchen
Full bath
Sleeps 4 to 6
Adaptable to being off the grid

WOODSTOVE: as a central design element, would be a nice place for a Franklin stove, which offers the charm of an open fire as well as heat.

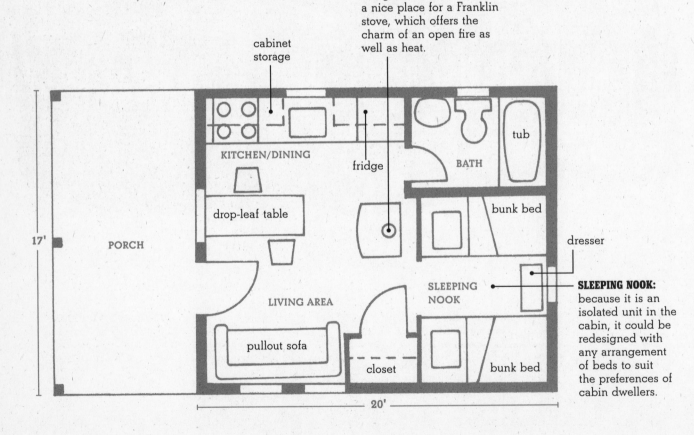

cabinet storage

KITCHEN/DINING

fridge

BATH

tub

drop-leaf table

bunk bed

dresser

17'

PORCH

LIVING AREA

SLEEPING NOOK

SLEEPING NOOK: because it is an isolated unit in the cabin, it could be redesigned with any arrangement of beds to suit the preferences of cabin dwellers.

pullout sofa

closet

bunk bed

20'

PITCHED ROOF: could support solar panels if oriented to the south.

PORCH: can be screened or open, or framed in as additional living space.

NATIVE ROCK: is an ideal building material, helping the cabin feel naturally sited in the surrounding environment; it also protects the building in damp areas or dense woods, where little drying occurs.

NATURAL FACING MATERIAL: such as stucco combines well with rock, lending a lighter feeling to the exterior.

FOUR-SEASON MINI CABIN

With central heat as well as a huge fireplace, this cabin is a cozy year-round retreat. The loft gives some privacy to the sleeping accommodations and allows the first floor to have an open stretch of floor space.

Features
348 square feet
Full kitchen
Full bath
Sleeps 2
Fireplace
Adaptable to being off the grid

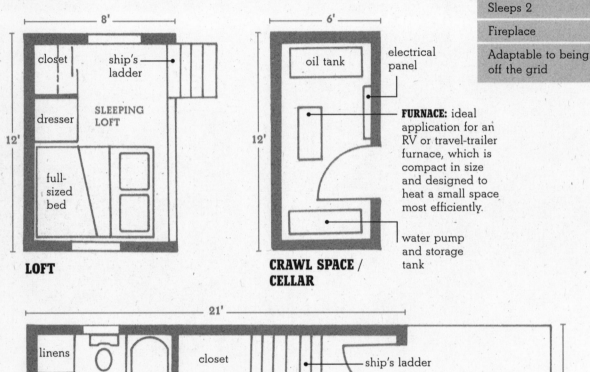

LOFT

CRAWL SPACE / CELLAR

FURNACE: ideal application for an RV or travel-trailer furnace, which is compact in size and designed to heat a small space most efficiently.

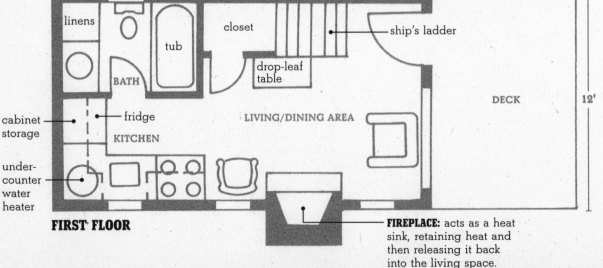

FIRST FLOOR

FIREPLACE: acts as a heat sink, retaining heat and then releasing it back into the living space.

PITCHED ROOF: could support solar panels if oriented to the south.

CELLAR OR CRAWL SPACE: can house not only the furnace but also a water pump and storage tank, an electrical service panel, and a fuel oil tank.

LOYAL SOCK CABIN

This cabin offers a lot in just more than 350 square feet, including a full bath and full kitchen. The outdoor storage locker is roomy, able to accommodate bulky gear for hunting, boating, or other outdoor activities. Its full structural framework, if coupled with a strong door and lock, allows it to be a secure storage site.

Features
352 square feet
Full kitchen
Full bath
Sleeps 2 or 3
Outside storage locker
Adaptable to being off the grid

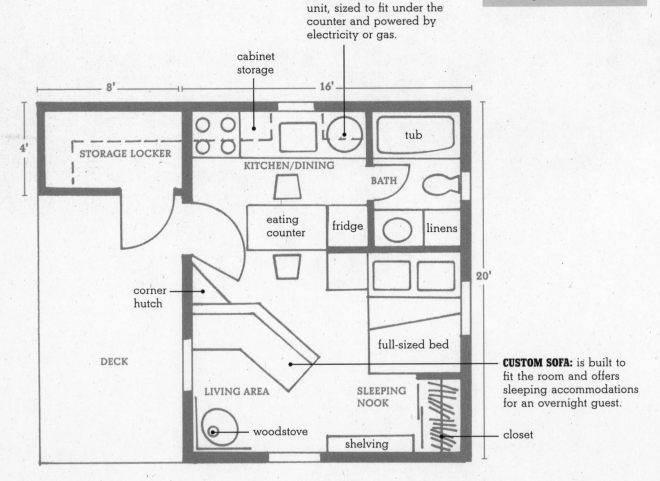

WATER HEATER: is an RV unit, sized to fit under the counter and powered by electricity or gas.

cabinet storage

8'   16'

4'

STORAGE LOCKER

KITCHEN/DINING

tub

BATH

eating counter

fridge

linens

20'

corner hutch

full-sized bed

CUSTOM SOFA: is built to fit the room and offers sleeping accommodations for an overnight guest.

DECK

LIVING AREA

SLEEPING NOOK

woodstove

shelving

closet

PITCHED ROOF: could
support solar panels if
oriented to the south.

DECK: could be converted
to an opened or screened
porch, or framed in as
additional living space.

WOODS CABIN IN THE ROUND

This semicircular cabin is designed to allow for maximum view of the outdoors. This cabin can be oriented to face south and capture the sun for passive solar heating.

Features

353 square feet

Full kitchen

Three-quarter bath

Sleeps 2 to 4

Adaptable to being off the grid

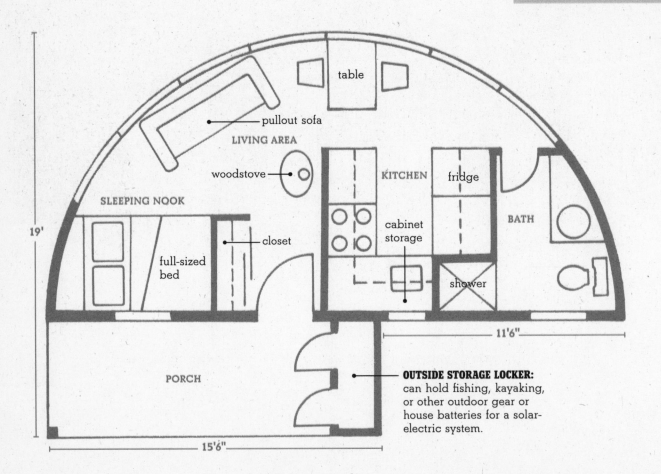

table

pullout sofa

LIVING AREA

woodstove

SLEEPING NOOK

KITCHEN

fridge

BATH

cabinet storage

closet

full-sized bed

shower

19'

11'6"

PORCH

OUTSIDE STORAGE LOCKER: can hold fishing, kayaking, or other outdoor gear or house batteries for a solar-electric system.

15'6"

PITCHED ROOF: could support solar panels if oriented to the south; alternatively, a freestanding solar-electric panel unit could be set up nearby.

WINDOW BANK: across the rounded front is designed to capture maximum view, helping the cabin feel open to the outdoors.

PORCH: can be open or screened, or could be framed in as additional living space.

OHIO PYLE CABIN

This cabin works well along a riverbank or stream. The piers support the structure well off the ground, protecting it from high spring water and allowing it to stay dry in damp conditions.

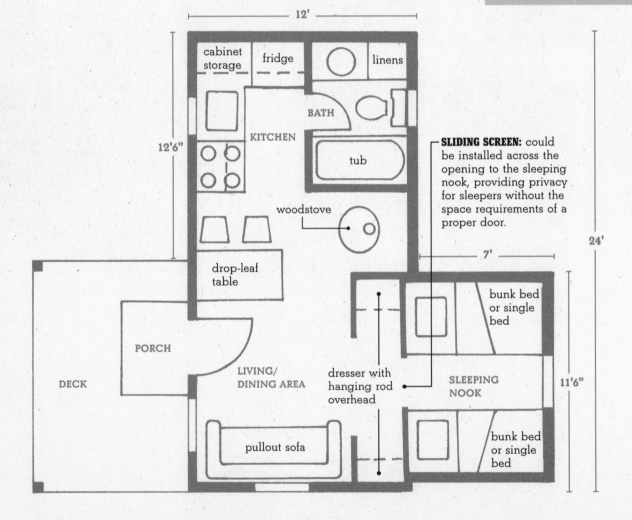

12'

cabinet storage   fridge   linens

12'6"   KITCHEN   BATH   tub

woodstove

drop-leaf table

SLIDING SCREEN: could be installed across the opening to the sleeping nook, providing privacy for sleepers without the space requirements of a proper door.

7'

bunk bed or single bed

24'

PORCH

DECK   LIVING/ DINING AREA

dresser with hanging rod overhead   SLEEPING NOOK   11'6"

pullout sofa   bunk bed or single bed

PITCHED ROOF: could support solar panels if oriented to the south.

ROOF OVER DOORWAY: makes an inviting entry, sheltering anyone at the door from inclement weather.

DECK: could easily be replaced with open or screened porch.

TRAILER-WIDE CABIN

Just the right size for a modular home trailer frame, this cabin is designed to be built off-site and trucked to the building site. Narrow cabins like this one are ideal for lakeside sites, where the lots tend to be long and deep but not very wide.

Features
372 square feet
Full kitchen
Full bath
Sleeps 2
Can be built off-site and trailered in
Adaptable to being off the grid

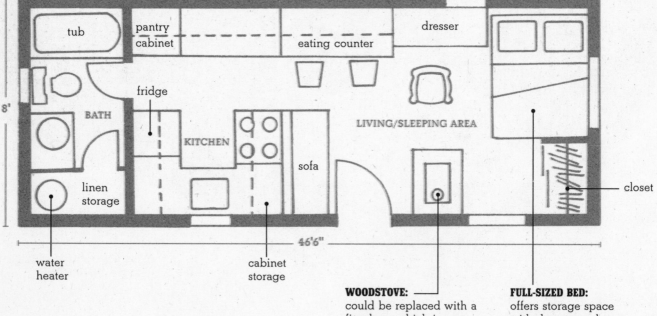

tub

pantry cabinet

dresser

eating counter

BATH

fridge

KITCHEN

LIVING/SLEEPING AREA

sofa

linen storage

closet

8'

46'6"

water heater

cabinet storage

WOODSTOVE: could be replaced with a fireplace, which is more romantic, if not quite as efficient at providing heat.

FULL-SIZED BED: offers storage space with drawers or boxes underneath.

PITCHED ROOF: could support solar panels if oriented to the south.

CLERESTORY WINDOWS AND SKYLIGHT: bring light to the interior and can be opened in warm weather for natural ventilation.

NARROW DIMENSIONS: allow the home to be built off-site on a modular home trailer frame, then trucked in to the building site.

ROUND HOUSE CABIN

A round cabin — how unique! Curved cement blocks are available for building cisterns and farm silos and adapt well to building round cabins. This design calls for a custom-built curved sofa and fold-up table to make the most of the interior space.

Features

380 square feet

Full kitchen

Full bath

Sleeps 2

Adaptable to being off the grid

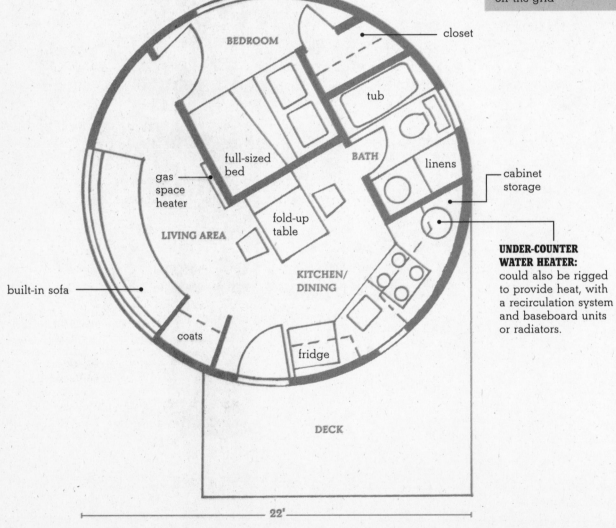

closet

BEDROOM

tub

full-sized bed

BATH

linens

gas space heater

cabinet storage

LIVING AREA

fold-up table

UNDER-COUNTER WATER HEATER: could also be rigged to provide heat, with a recirculation system and baseboard units or radiators.

built-in sofa

KITCHEN/ DINING

coats

fridge

DECK

22'

UPPER WINDOWS: should face the prevailing view, helping the cabin feel open to the outdoors.

PITCHED ROOF: could support solar panels if oriented to the south.

DECK: could be framed in as a porch or interior living space, squaring off one corner of the cabin.

LAKESIDE MINI CABIN

To be lakeside in the summer! This design lends itself well to the typically narrow width of lakeside lots. The angled front provides for a view of the water.

FULL-SIZED BED: offers storage space with a shelf over the foot of the bed and drawers or boxes underneath.

FRONT DOOR: could be equipped with a patio sliding door to increase the view from the inside.

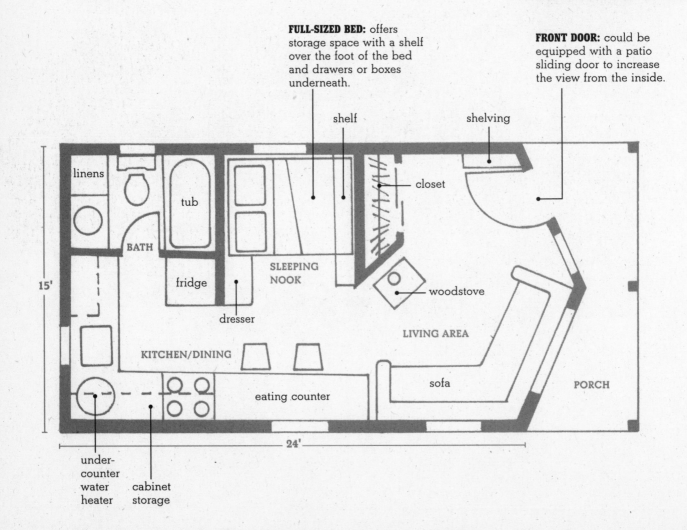

linens

tub

shelf

shelving

closet

BATH

fridge

SLEEPING NOOK

woodstove

dresser

LIVING AREA

15'

KITCHEN/DINING

sofa

PORCH

eating counter

24'

under-counter water heater

cabinet storage

CLERESTORY WINDOWS:
bring light to the interior
and can be opened in
warm weather for natural
ventilation.

PITCHED ROOF: could
support solar panels if
oriented to the south.

PORCH: could be
augmented with
a lakeside deck.

WEDGE CABIN

This mini cabin has the feel of a much larger one. It features an unusually large amount of glass, making it feel light and airy. It can be oriented toward a great view or toward the south for passive solar heating.

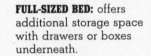

Features
384 square feet
Full kitchen
Three-quarter bath
Sleeps 2 to 4
Fireplace
Adaptable to being off the grid

MASSIVE FIELDSTONE FIREPLACE: anchors the living area and acts as a heat sink, retaining heat and then releasing it back into the living space.

FULL-SIZED BED: offers additional storage space with drawers or boxes underneath.

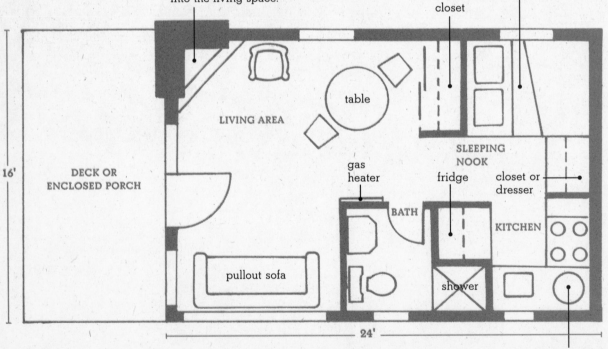

closet

DECK OR ENCLOSED PORCH

16'

LIVING AREA

table

gas heater

BATH

SLEEPING NOOK

fridge

closet or dresser

KITCHEN

pullout sofa

shower

24'

under-counter water heater

PORCH OPTION: can be added, in which case clerestory windows would be added to the upper porch wall.

PITCHED ROOF: could support solar panels if oriented to the south.

FURNACE CREEK CABIN

This 399-square-foot cabin has some surprising amenities, including a full-sized kitchen and bath and a private bedroom. Cabin lovers who also appreciate the amenities of home will enjoy this design.

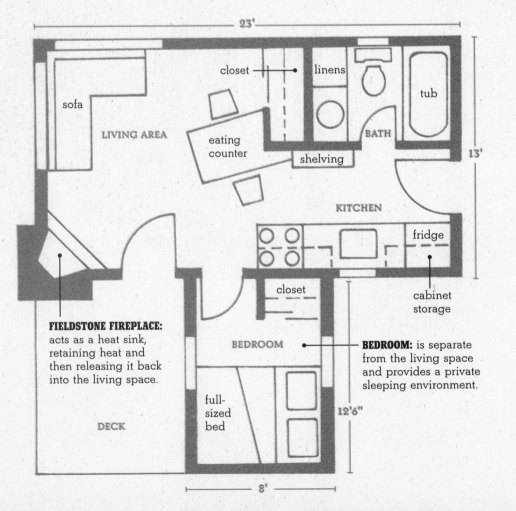

FIELDSTONE FIREPLACE: acts as a heat sink, retaining heat and then releasing it back into the living space.

BEDROOM: is separate from the living space and provides a private sleeping environment.

PITCHED ROOF: could support solar panels if oriented to the south.

DECK: could also be framed in as a porch or additional living space.

TRAILERABLE MINI CABIN

Designed to be built off-site and trucked to the cabin site, this mini cabin can be built as a winter project — perhaps by the whole family — and enjoyed during the summer. The shallow roofline won't interfere with electrical wires during transportation.

Features

408 square feet

Full kitchen

Full bath

Sleeps 2 to 6

Can be built off-site and trailered in

Adaptable to being off the grid

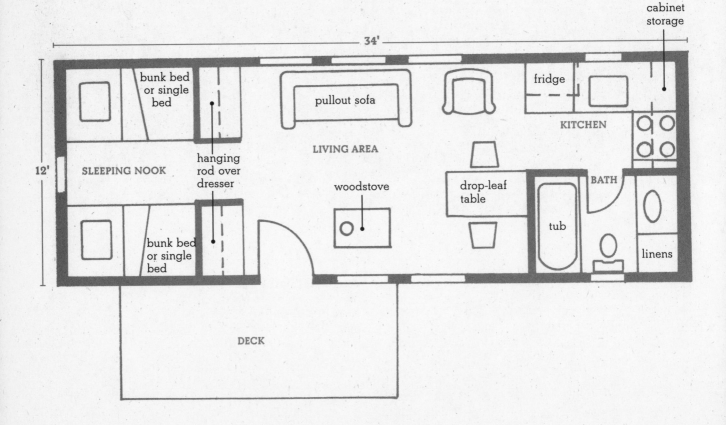

ROOFLINE: on either side could support solar panels if oriented to the south.

NARROW DIMENSIONS: allow the cabin to be trailered to the building site and are ideal for the typically narrow lakeside lots.

DECK: could be extended to run across the length of the cabin, or framed in as an open or screened porch.

LITTLE PINE CREEK CABIN

Fishing is all the more fun with a comfortable cabin waiting at the end of the day. This classic fishing cabin is ideal for a small family or a couple of fishing buddies. The fireplace provides heating and the ambience of a roaring fire on cold evenings.

Features
414 square feet
Full kitchen
Full bath
Sleeps 2 to 4
Fireplace
Adaptable to being off the grid

FIELDSTONE FIREPLACE: acts as a heat sink, retaining heat and then releasing it back into the living space.

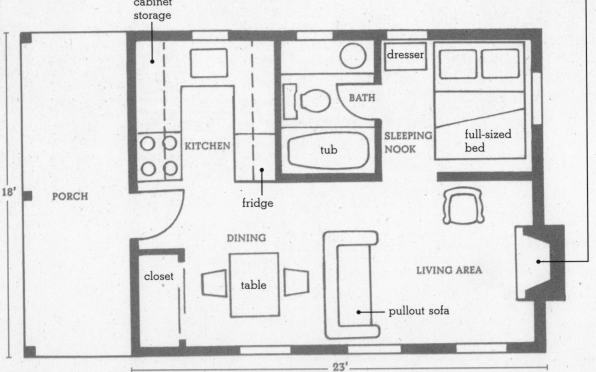

PITCHED ROOF: could support solar panels if oriented to the south.

CLERESTORY WINDOWS: could be added to bring light to the interior and allow for natural ventilation in warm weather.

PORCH: can be open or screened, or could be framed in as additional living space.

RICKETS GLEN CABIN

This mini cabin design features a cathedral ceiling framed on one side with banks of overhead windows, allowing the interior to feel spacious and bright. More windows could easily be added to the deck wall, helping the cabin feel even more open to the outside.

DECK WALL: could have windows added, making the deck space seem more integral to the interior living space.

FREESTANDING FIELDSTONE FIREPLACE: acts as a heat sink, retaining heat and then releasing it back into the living space.

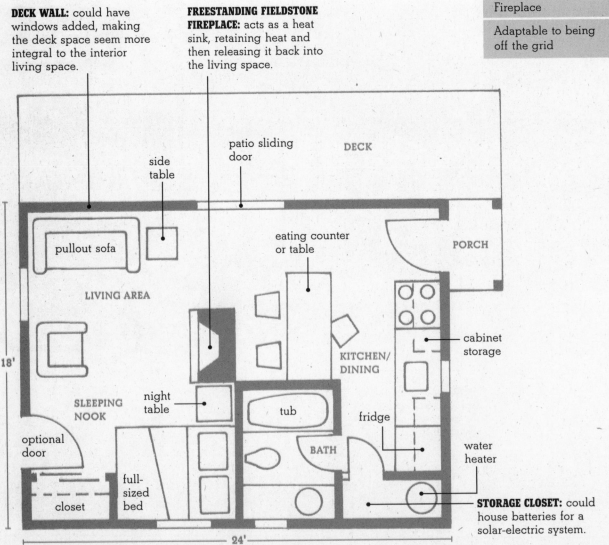

patio sliding door

DECK

side table

eating counter or table

PORCH

pullout sofa

LIVING AREA

cabinet storage

KITCHEN/DINING

night table

tub

fridge

SLEEPING NOOK

water heater

optional door

BATH

full-sized bed

STORAGE CLOSET: could house batteries for a solar-electric system.

closet

18'

24'

PITCHED ROOF: could support solar panels if oriented to the south.

CLERESTORY WINDOWS: bring light to the interior and can be opened in warm weather for natural ventilation.

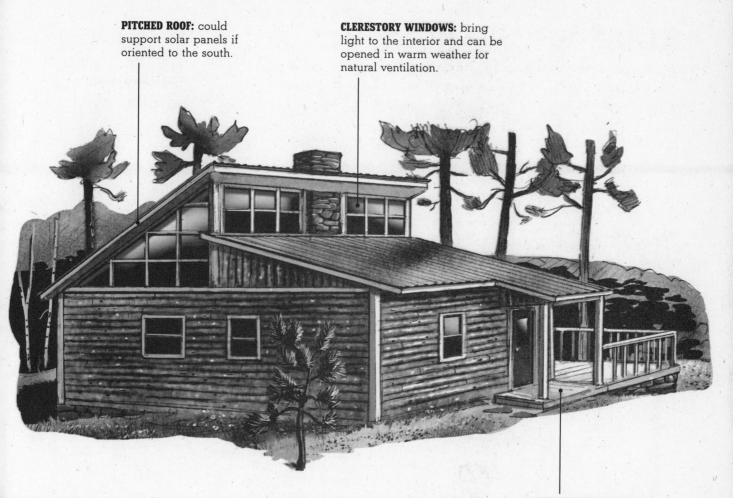

DECK: can be converted to an open or screened porch, or framed in as additional living space.

GLASS HOUSE CABIN

The design of this cabin lends itself to the usually narrow dimensions of lakeside lots. The glass front is equipped with patio sliding doors to increase the view.

Features
434 square feet
Full kitchen
Full bath
Sleeps 2 to 4
Designed for passive solar heating

WATER HEATER: can be coupled with baseboard units or radiators to provide space heating.

BATHROOM: is designed to accommodate a spa tub, an unusual but welcome amenity in any cabin design.

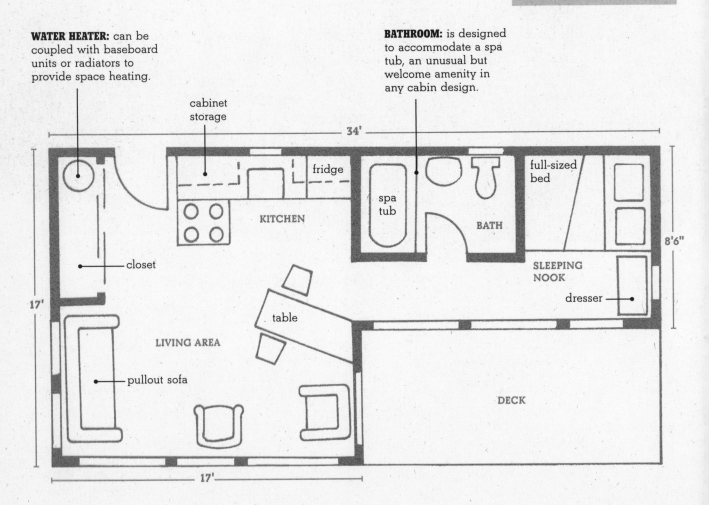

cabinet storage

34'

fridge

full-sized bed

spa tub

KITCHEN

BATH

8'6"

closet

SLEEPING NOOK

17'

dresser

table

LIVING AREA

pullout sofa

DECK

17'

PITCHED ROOF: could
support solar panels if
oriented to the south.

GLASS FRONT: can be
oriented to the south to
provide passive solar
heating.

**TWO SETS OF PATIO SLIDING
DOORS:** complement the
glass front of this cabin
and accentuate the view
from the inside.

DECK: could easily be
converted to a porch or
framed in as additional
living space.

MODIFIED A-FRAME CABIN

A-frame cabins typically have usable-space problems, since the roof meets the floor at an angle. This design modifies the roofline on one side to expand the usable space, helping the interior feel open rather than cramped.

SLEEPING LOFT: is accessible by a standard staircase and features skylights, which bring in natural light and can be opened for ventilation.

HOT WATER HEATER: under the stairs could be coupled with baseboard units or radiators to provide space heating.

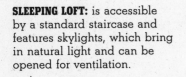

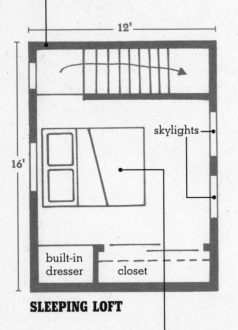

12'

16'

skylights

built-in dresser

closet

SLEEPING LOFT

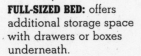

FULL-SIZED BED: offers additional storage space with drawers or boxes underneath.

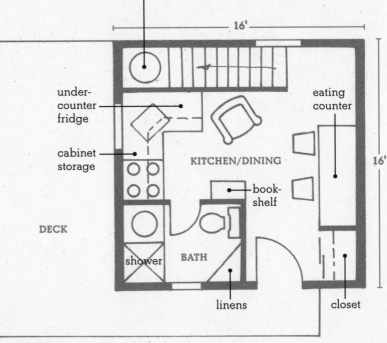

16'

16'

under-counter fridge

cabinet storage

eating counter

KITCHEN/DINING

book-shelf

DECK

shower

BATH

linens

closet

FIRST FLOOR

ROOFLINE: is ideal for supporting solar panels; should be oriented to the south to maximize sun exposure.

operable skylights

WRAPAROUND DECK: is a great space for outdoor living, with plenty of room for seating, tables, and even a grill.

TWO-STORY LAKESIDE CABIN

This two-story cabin is designed with a small footprint to fit narrow lakeside lots. It offers the luxury of a queen-sized bed in the second-floor bedroom, which is accessed by an elegant squared spiral staircase.

Features
450 square feet
Full kitchen
Three-quarter bath
Sleeps 2 to 4
Two full stories
Adaptable to being off the grid

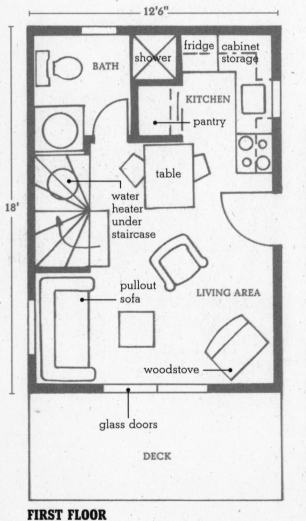

FIRST FLOOR

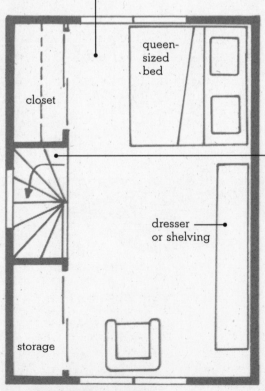

SECOND-STORY BEDROOM: has room for a reading chair, making it a wonderful quiet retreat in daytime as well as nighttime.

SQUARED SPIRAL STAIRCASE: is an elegant functional feature and can be dressed up or down depending on the type of milling used for the banister and railings.

SECOND-FLOOR BEDROOM

PITCHED ROOF: could support solar panels if either side is oriented to the south.

GLASS DOORS: face out to the deck, letting in plenty of light and helping the first floor feel open to the outdoors.

YURT CABIN

Patterned after the domed tents favored by nomads of central Asia, this round cabin is built on deck foundation and features a skylight at its apex. Its wall panels can be built off-site and then trucked in and assembled.

Features
452 square feet
Full kitchen
Three-quarter bath
Sleeps 2 or 3
Can be built partially off-site and trailered in

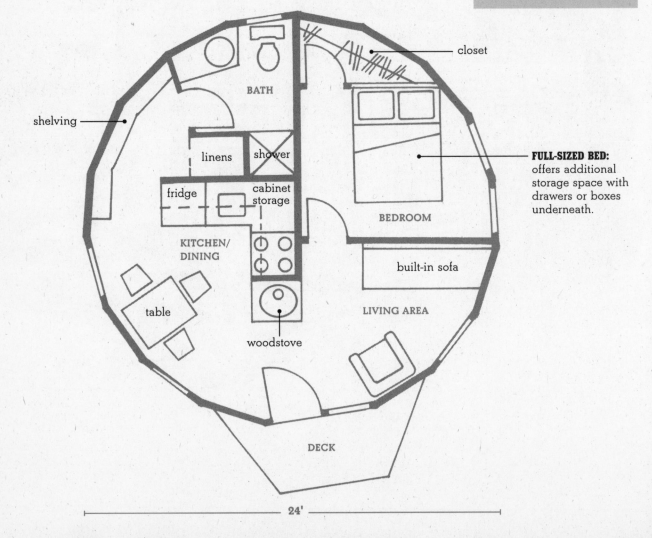

shelving

closet

BATH

linens

shower

FULL-SIZED BED: offers additional storage space with drawers or boxes underneath.

fridge

cabinet storage

BEDROOM

KITCHEN/ DINING

built-in sofa

table

LIVING AREA

woodstove

DECK

24'

CENTRAL SKYLIGHT: allows light into the cabin's center and can be opened in warm weather for natural ventilation.

WALL AND ROOF SECTIONS: can be built off-site and then trucked to the site and assembled, forming the shell of the cabin.

FOUNDATION: can be as simple as decking built over piers; airflow underneath the cabin will aid in ventilation and moisture control.

POCONO PINES CABIN

This design is ideal for a weekend cabin. Contemporary design concepts make it feel and function like a much bigger cabin. Designed for a location with a great view, one of the walls of the living space incorporates three patio sliding doors that open to the deck.

Features
455 square feet
Full kitchen
Full bath
Sleeps 2 to 4
Fireplace
Adaptable to being off the grid

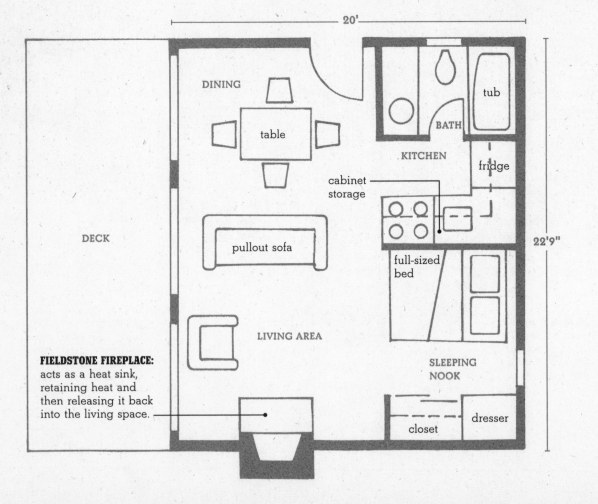

20'

22'9"

DINING

table

tub

BATH

KITCHEN

fridge

cabinet storage

DECK

pullout sofa

full-sized bed

LIVING AREA

SLEEPING NOOK

FIELDSTONE FIREPLACE: acts as a heat sink, retaining heat and then releasing it back into the living space.

closet

dresser

UPPER-LEVEL ROUND WINDOW: serves as a design focal point, bringing natural light across the cathedral ceiling.

PITCHED ROOF: could support solar panels if one side is oriented to the south.

DECK: can be converted to an open or screened porch or framed in as additional living space.

PATIO SLIDING DOORS: can be oriented toward a great view or to the south for passive solar gain.

QUONSET CABIN

The Quonset is back! A Quonset hut constructed on top of a low masonry or frame wall is a fast way to build a cabin. This design is based on a traditional 15-foot-wide Quonset hut, but it is easily adaptable to other Quonset-hut-like buildings.

Features
480 square feet
Full kitchen
Full bath
Sleeps 2 to 4
Utilizes one 15-foot-wide Quonset hut

closet

cabinet storage

under-counter water heater

BATHROOM WALLS: extend to just 8 feet in height, allowing light and air into the windowless room.

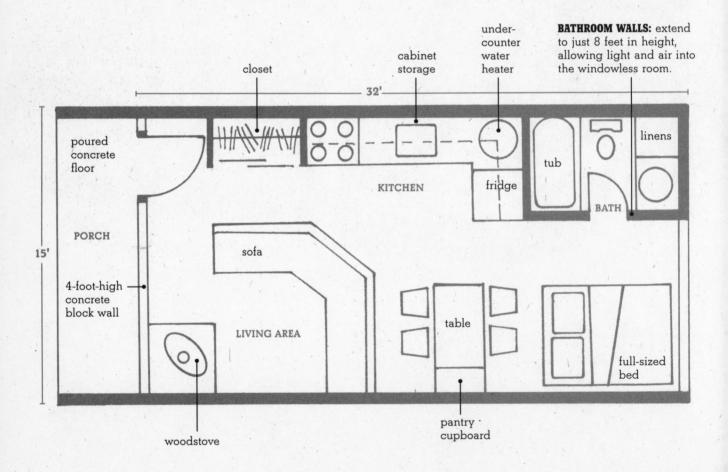

32'

poured concrete floor

KITCHEN

fridge

tub

linens

BATH

15'

PORCH

4-foot-high concrete block wall

sofa

LIVING AREA

table

full-sized bed

woodstove

pantry cupboard

FOUR-FOOT OVERHANG: provides shade for the porch, while still allowing ambient light to penetrate the cabin interior.

LARGE SKYLIGHT: allows additional light into the cabin and can be opened in warm weather for natural ventilation.

MASONRY WALLS AND GALVANIZED SHEATHING: create a no-maintenance cabin exterior.

OPEN FLOOR PLAN AND WINDOWS IN END WALLS: allow a lot of light into what is usually a dark interior.

OPEN-LIVING MINI CABIN

This cabin is based on an open space concept, making it function like a much larger cabin. Separating the two beds with the bathroom offers each a degree of privacy.

TWO SLEEPING NOOKS: provide some privacy for occupants, rather than having the beds doubled up in a single sleeping space.

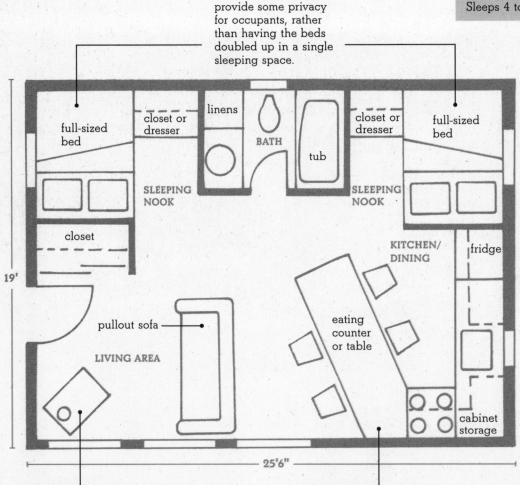

full-sized bed

closet or dresser

linens

BATH

tub

closet or dresser

full-sized bed

SLEEPING NOOK

SLEEPING NOOK

closet

KITCHEN/ DINING

fridge

pullout sofa

eating counter or table

LIVING AREA

cabinet storage

19'

25'6"

WOODSTOVE: could easily be replaced with a fireplace, which offers greater ambience though not as much heat.

DINING TABLE: could have stools that tuck underneath, so the table doubles as an island counter for the kitchen.

PITCHED ROOF: could
support solar panels,
especially if oriented
to the south.

ENTRYWAY: could easily
be expanded to a large
deck or porch.

JEAN'S RUN CABIN

This cabin sleeps six people in just more than 500 square feet. The Murphy bed and dining table both can be folded up against the wall to increase the usable interior space, while the loft is accessible by a narrow-profile ship's ladder.

Features
501 square feet
Full kitchen
Three-quarter bath
Sleeps 4 to 6
Adaptable to being off the grid

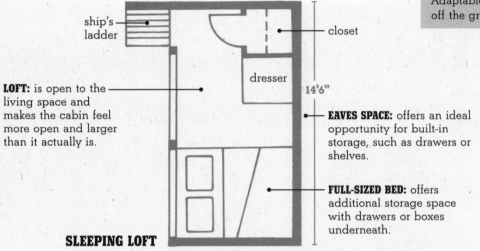

ship's ladder

6'6"

closet

dresser

14'6"

LOFT: is open to the living space and makes the cabin feel more open and larger than it actually is.

EAVES SPACE: offers an ideal opportunity for built-in storage, such as drawers or shelves.

FULL-SIZED BED: offers additional storage space with drawers or boxes underneath.

SLEEPING LOFT

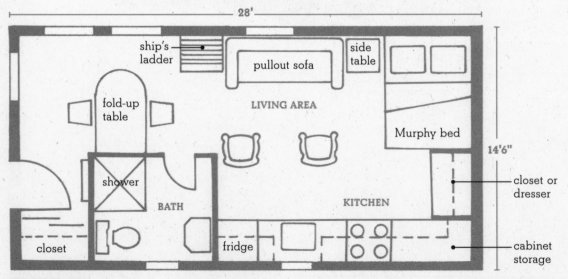

28'

ship's ladder

pullout sofa

side table

LIVING AREA

fold-up table

Murphy bed

14'6"

shower

closet or dresser

BATH

KITCHEN

closet

fridge

cabinet storage

FIRST FLOOR

CLERESTORY WINDOWS: bring light to the interior and can be opened in warm weather for natural ventilation.

PITCHED ROOF: could support solar panels if oriented to the south.

PINE CREEK CABIN

Based on the saltbox houses found in New England, this cabin design features an open sleeping loft that overlooks the living space, accessible via a set of steep stairs. Since warm air rises, very little heat is needed to keep occupants warm at night.

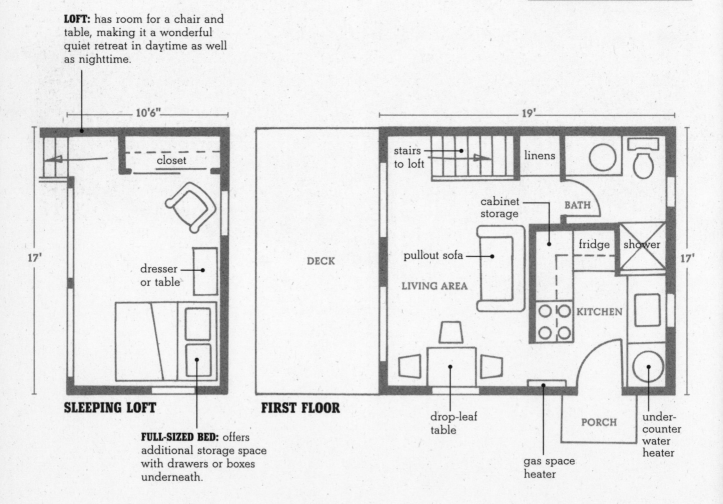

LOFT: has room for a chair and table, making it a wonderful quiet retreat in daytime as well as nighttime.

10'6"

closet

17'

dresser or table

SLEEPING LOFT

FULL-SIZED BED: offers additional storage space with drawers or boxes underneath.

19'

stairs to loft

linens

cabinet storage

BATH

DECK

pullout sofa

fridge

shower

LIVING AREA

17'

KITCHEN

FIRST FLOOR

drop-leaf table

PORCH

under-counter water heater

gas space heater

PATIO SLIDING DOOR:
opens onto the deck;
if oriented to the south
it would provide passive
solar heating.

ROOFLINE: is ideal for
supporting solar panels,
especially if oriented to
the south.

operable skylights

A CABIN FOR TWO

A cabin with a spa tub? Absolutely. With the addition of a fireplace and a full-sized sleeping nook complete with built-ins, it is a romantic retreat for two — though it also offers accommodations for guests or kids with a pullout sofa.

Features
513 square feet
Full kitchen
Full bath
Sleeps 2 to 4
Fireplace
Adaptable to being off the grid

BATHROOM: is designed to accommodate a spa tub, an unusual but welcome amenity in any cabin design.

FIELDSTONE FIREPLACE: is a focal point of the living area and acts as a heat sink, retaining heat and then releasing it back into the living space.

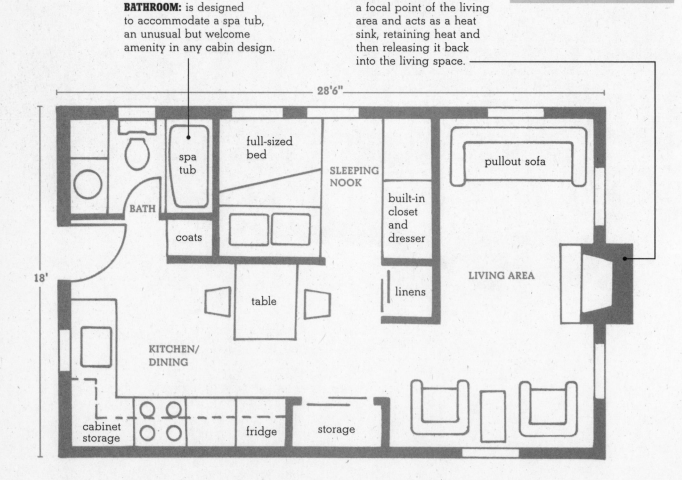

PITCHED ROOF: could support solar panels if one side is oriented to the south.

CATHEDRAL CEILING: makes the cabin feel bigger than it is.

LONG, VERTICAL WINDOWS: frame the fireplace and offer a good outdoor view from the living area; orienting these windows to the south would give the cabin passive solar heating.

FIREPLACE CABIN

Who doesn't like to sit around a fire on a cool evening? The focal point of this cabin is the massive stone fireplace, which anchors the living and dining space and is framed by banks of windows.

Features

570 square feet

Full kitchen

Full bath

Sleeps 2 to 4

Fireplace

Adaptable to being off the grid

FIELDSTONE FIREPLACE: acts as a heat sink, retaining heat and then releasing it back into the living space.

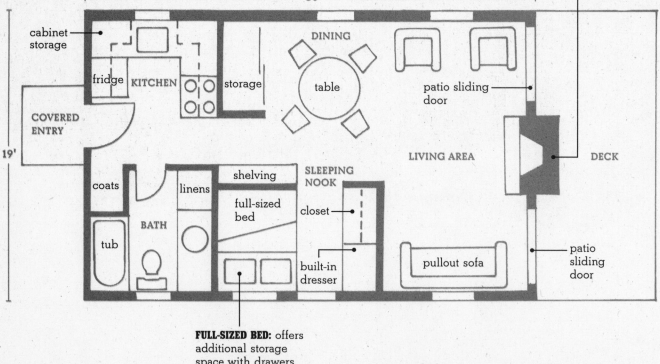

cabinet storage

fridge

KITCHEN

storage

COVERED ENTRY

DINING

table

patio sliding door

LIVING AREA

DECK

19'

30'

coats

linens

shelving

full-sized bed

SLEEPING NOOK

closet

BATH

tub

built-in dresser

pullout sofa

patio sliding door

FULL-SIZED BED: offers additional storage space with drawers or boxes underneath.

PITCHED ROOF: could support solar panels if either side is oriented to the south.

HIGH BANKS OF WINDOW: bring natural light across the cathedral ceiling, helping the cabin feel open and airy.

RECTANGULAR FOOTPRINT: lends itself to narrow lakeside lots.

SPRING CREEK CABIN

This cabin offers the privacy of a separate bedroom; in combination with the pullout sofa, it can accommodate two couples. The glass of the entrance door wall offers a good view of the outdoors from the living area. Orienting these windows to the south would allow them to contribute to passive solar heating.

Features
576 square feet
Full kitchen
Full bath
Sleeps 2 to 4
Adaptable to being off the grid

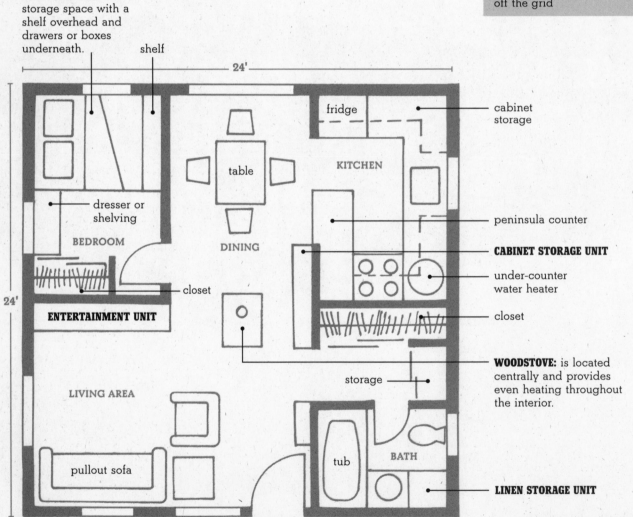

FULL-SIZED BED: offers storage space with a shelf overhead and drawers or boxes underneath.

shelf

24'

24'

cabinet storage

fridge

KITCHEN

table

dresser or shelving

BEDROOM

DINING

peninsula counter

CABINET STORAGE UNIT

under-counter water heater

closet

closet

ENTERTAINMENT UNIT

WOODSTOVE: is located centrally and provides even heating throughout the interior.

storage

LIVING AREA

pullout sofa

tub

BATH

LINEN STORAGE UNIT

PITCHED ROOF: could support solar panels if oriented to the south.

HIGH BANKS OF WINDOWS: bring natural light across the cathedral ceiling, helping the cabin feel open and airy.

ENTERTAINMENT UNIT

LINEN STORAGE UNIT

CABINET STORAGE UNIT

CLERESTORY CABIN WITH DINING ROOM

This classic clerestory design employs a massive fieldstone fireplace for space heating. Unlike most other plans, it also features a separate dining space, perfect for cabin owners who appreciate a good sit-down meal.

Features
584 square feet
Full kitchen
Full bath
Sleeps 3 to 6
Fireplace
Adaptable to being off the grid

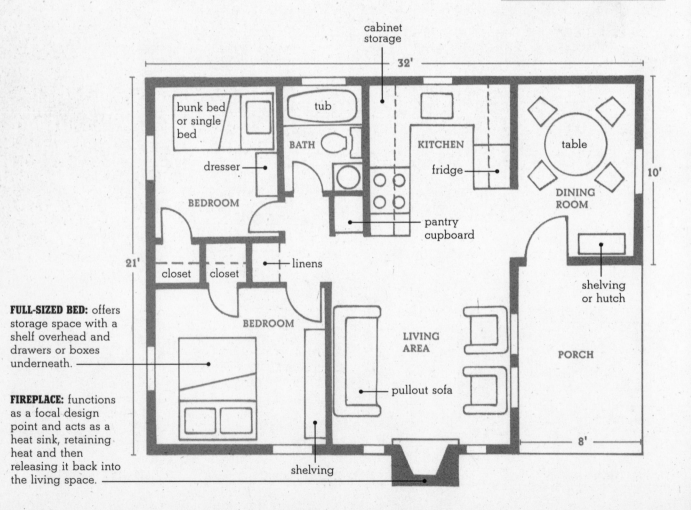

cabinet storage

32'

bunk bed or single bed

tub

KITCHEN

table

dresser

BATH

fridge

10'

BEDROOM

DINING ROOM

pantry cupboard

21'

linens

closet   closet

shelving or hutch

FULL-SIZED BED: offers storage space with a shelf overhead and drawers or boxes underneath.

BEDROOM

LIVING AREA

PORCH

FIREPLACE: functions as a focal design point and acts as a heat sink, retaining heat and then releasing it back into the living space.

pullout sofa

8'

shelving

PITCHED ROOF: could support solar panels if oriented to the south.

CLERESTORY WINDOWS: bring light to the interior and can be opened in warm weather for natural ventilation.

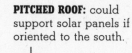

PORCH: could be incorporated into the living area or dining room to add to the usable interior space.

SUNROOM CABIN

The central sunroom of this cabin creates passive solar heating — and possibly a great view. It also adds flexible additional living space connected to the rest of the cabin by patio sliding doors.

Features
594 square feet
Full kitchen
Full bath
Sleeps 2 or 3
Designed for passive solar heating

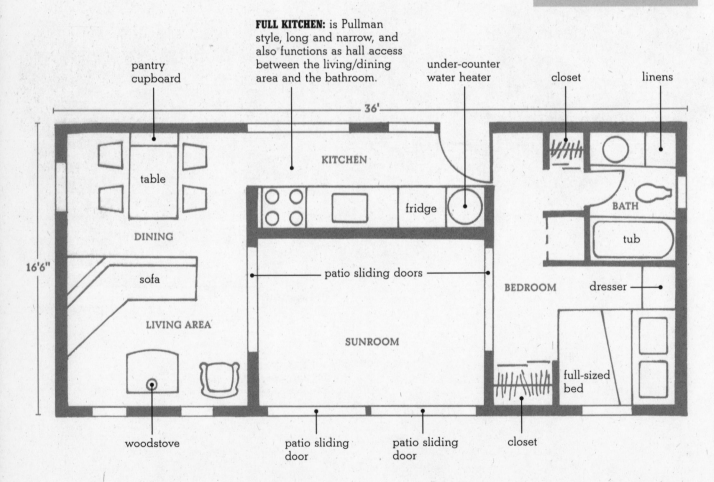

pantry cupboard

FULL KITCHEN: is Pullman style, long and narrow, and also functions as hall access between the living/dining area and the bathroom.

under-counter water heater

closet

linens

36'

KITCHEN

table

fridge

BATH

DINING

tub

16'6"

sofa

patio sliding doors

BEDROOM

dresser

LIVING AREA

SUNROOM

full-sized bed

woodstove

patio sliding door

patio sliding door

closet

INSULATED GLASS PANELS: in end walls let in loads of light and make the cabin feel bigger than it is.

polycarbonate light panel

WINDOWS IN THE LIVING AREA: begin at floor level, opening the interior to the great outdoors.

SLIDING SUNROOM DOORS: can be left open to circulate heat from the sunroom to the rest of the cabin.

BAJA CABIN

This design features two private bedrooms separated from the rest of the living space by a sunroom. The sunroom itself is a flexible space, able to accommodate another pullout sofa for additional sleeping space.

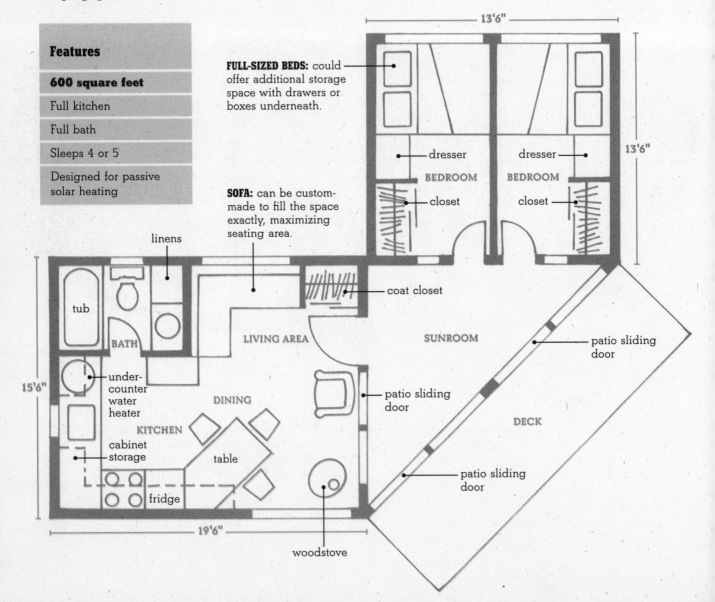

Features

600 square feet

Full kitchen

Full bath

Sleeps 4 or 5

Designed for passive solar heating

FULL-SIZED BEDS: could offer additional storage space with drawers or boxes underneath.

SOFA: can be custom-made to fill the space exactly, maximizing seating area.

linens

13'6"

dresser

dresser

13'6"

BEDROOM

BEDROOM

closet

closet

coat closet

tub

BATH

LIVING AREA

SUNROOM

patio sliding door

under-counter water heater

DINING

15'6"

KITCHEN

patio sliding door

cabinet storage

table

DECK

fridge

patio sliding door

19'6"

woodstove

SLIDING SUNROOM DOORS: can be left open to circulate heat from the sunroom to the rest of the cabin.

DECK: is designed to fit across the sunroom exposure but can be expanded; it also can be replaced with a patio of brick or flagstone.

POCONOS CABIN

With a feel more like that of a house than a cabin, this design offers a private sleeping floor complete with its own half bath. The first floor has room for a large dining table and sectional sofa, making it a nice spot for hanging out even on a rainy day.

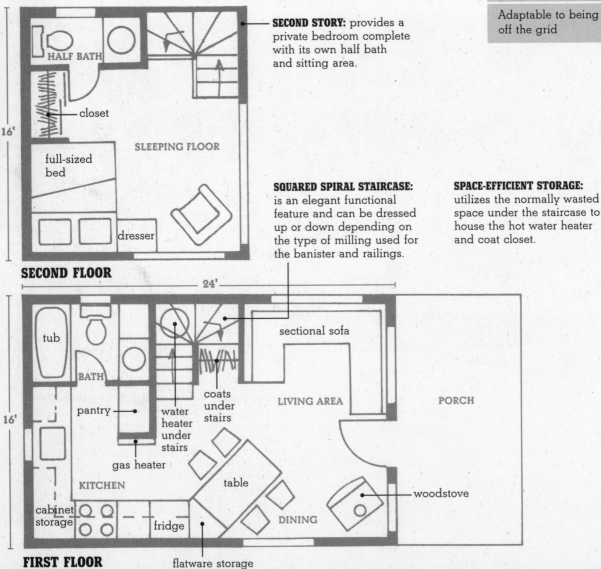

14'6"

HALF BATH

closet

16'

SLEEPING FLOOR

full-sized bed

dresser

SECOND FLOOR

SECOND STORY: provides a private bedroom complete with its own half bath and sitting area.

SQUARED SPIRAL STAIRCASE: is an elegant functional feature and can be dressed up or down depending on the type of milling used for the banister and railings.

SPACE-EFFICIENT STORAGE: utilizes the normally wasted space under the staircase to house the hot water heater and coat closet.

24'

tub

BATH

pantry

water heater under stairs

coats under stairs

sectional sofa

LIVING AREA

PORCH

16'

gas heater

table

KITCHEN

woodstove

cabinet storage

fridge

DINING

FIRST FLOOR

flatware storage

CLERESTORY WINDOWS: allow light into the second floor and can be opened in warm weather for natural ventilation.

PITCHED ROOF: could support solar panels if either side is oriented to the south.

PORCH: could be screened to keep out bugs or framed in as additional living space.

ENDLESS MOUNTAIN VIEW CABIN

Most of the windows in this design are grouped on one side, with the purpose of focusing the view from the inside on a particularly good vista. Orienting that wall to face south would also yield passive solar heating.

WALL OF WINDOWS: is designed to capture a particularly good view, allowing it to be admired from the main bedroom, living room, dining table, and kitchen.

WOODSTOVE: could be replaced with a fireplace for added ambience, allowing cabin dwellers to enjoy a roaring open fire on colder days.

FULL-SIZED BED: could offer additional storage space with drawers or boxes underneath.

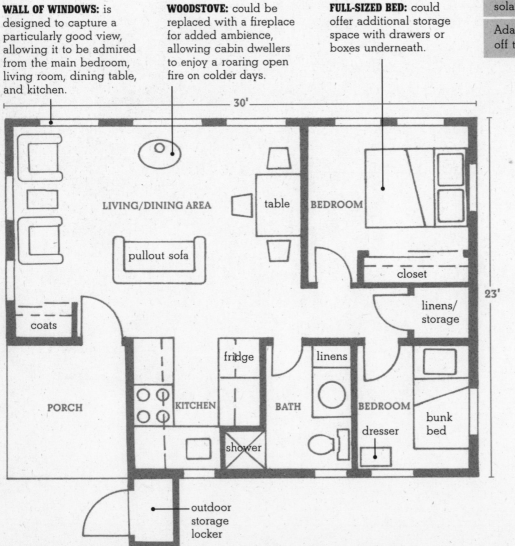

PITCHED ROOF: could support solar panels if either side is oriented to the south.

PORCH: could easily have a deck attached to it, extending the usable outdoor floor space.

GLASS-FRONT BEACH HOUSE

The living space of this cabin is, essentially, a glassed-in room. The walls of windows offer a great view, and orienting the windows to the south can add passive solar heating. This is an ideal application for the beach or along a lakefront.

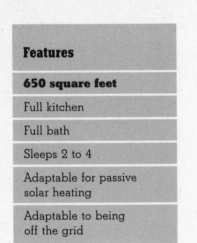

Features
650 square feet
Full kitchen
Full bath
Sleeps 2 to 4
Adaptable for passive solar heating
Adaptable to being off the grid

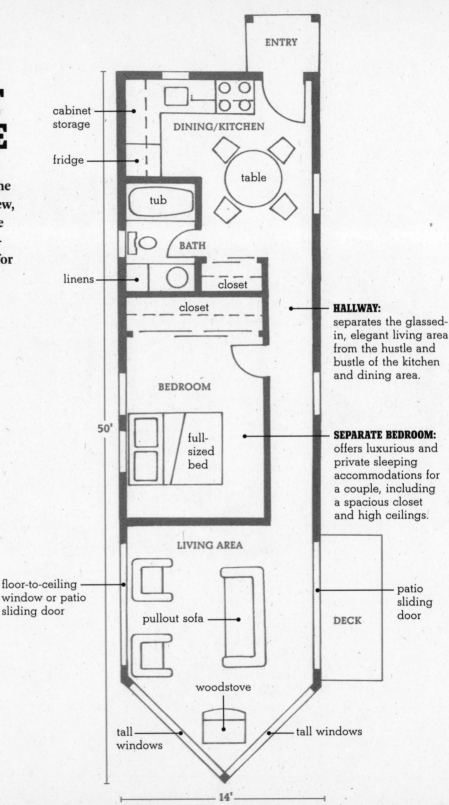

cabinet storage

fridge

linens

ENTRY

DINING/KITCHEN

table

tub

BATH

closet

closet

BEDROOM

full-sized bed

50'

LIVING AREA

floor-to-ceiling window or patio sliding door

pullout sofa

DECK

patio sliding door

woodstove

tall windows

tall windows

14'

HALLWAY: separates the glassed-in, elegant living area from the hustle and bustle of the kitchen and dining area.

SEPARATE BEDROOM: offers luxurious and private sleeping accommodations for a couple, including a spacious closet and high ceilings.

GLASS FRONT: transforms the living space into an open-to-the-outdoors lounge, with a 180-degree view.

PITCHED ROOF: could support solar panels if either side is oriented to the south.

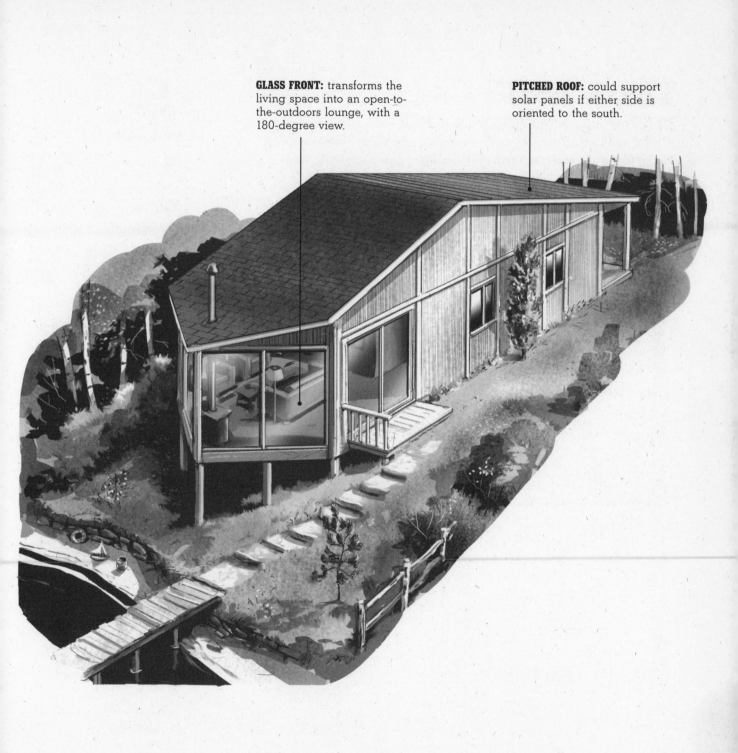

THE CLASSIC

This design offers all the classic cabin features, such as a fireplace, private bedrooms, and a compact but full kitchen and bathroom. It also features a spa tub, a real pleasure after a long day of fly fishing in a cold stream or hiking in the woods.

Features		
680 square feet		
Full kitchen		
Full bath		
Sleeps 4 to 6		
Fireplace		
Adaptable to being off the grid		

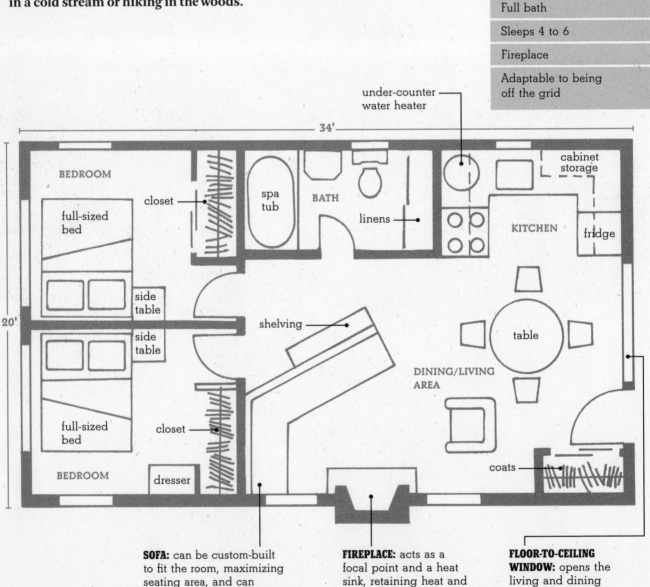

34'

20'

under-counter water heater

BEDROOM

closet

full-sized bed

side table

side table

full-sized bed

closet

dresser

BEDROOM

spa tub

BATH

linens

shelving

cabinet storage

KITCHEN

fridge

table

DINING/LIVING AREA

coats

SOFA: can be custom-built to fit the room, maximizing seating area, and can sleep up to two additional people.

FIREPLACE: acts as a focal point and a heat sink, retaining heat and then releasing it back into the living space.

FLOOR-TO-CEILING WINDOW: opens the living and dining area to the outdoors, bringing in light and offering a great view.

PITCHED ROOF: could support solar panels if oriented to the south.

FLOOR-TO-CEILING WINDOWS: off the two bedrooms help occupants feel embedded in the outdoors.

DOUBLE-DECKER BEACH HOUSE

This long, narrow layout is ideal for typically narrow lots found along beaches or lakefronts. The design also offers a great view from decks on both the living and sleeping levels.

Features

700 square feet

Full kitchen

One and a half baths

Sleeps 4 to 6

Adaptable to being off the grid

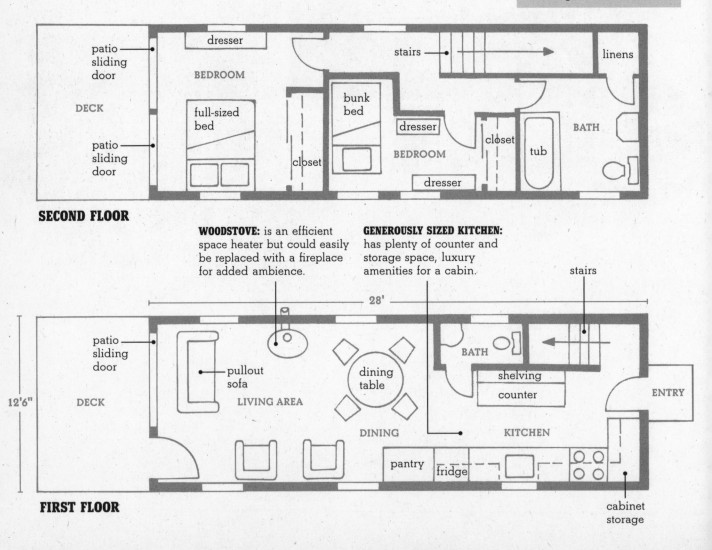

patio sliding door

DECK

patio sliding door

dresser

BEDROOM

full-sized bed

closet

bunk bed

dresser

BEDROOM

dresser

stairs

closet

tub

linens

BATH

SECOND FLOOR

WOODSTOVE: is an efficient space heater but could easily be replaced with a fireplace for added ambience.

GENEROUSLY SIZED KITCHEN: has plenty of counter and storage space, luxury amenities for a cabin.

stairs

28'

patio sliding door

12'6"

DECK

pullout sofa

LIVING AREA

dining table

DINING

BATH

shelving

counter

KITCHEN

ENTRY

pantry

fridge

cabinet storage

FIRST FLOOR

FULL SECOND STORY: serves as a private sleeping floor, with two bedrooms and a full bath.

PITCHED ROOF: could support solar panels if either side is oriented to the south.

DOUBLE DECKS: offer a great view from both levels of the cabin, with patio sliding doors providing access and bringing light to the interior; orienting these doors to the south would yield passive solar heating.

LAUREL MOUNTAIN CABIN

This cabin has a glassed-in porch accessible from the living space through a patio sliding door. This setup offers a great view of the outdoors from the main living area. If oriented to the south, it also allows passive solar heating.

Features

703 square feet

Full kitchen

Full bath

Sleeps 2 to 5

Fireplace insert

Designed for passive solar heating

Adaptable to being off the grid

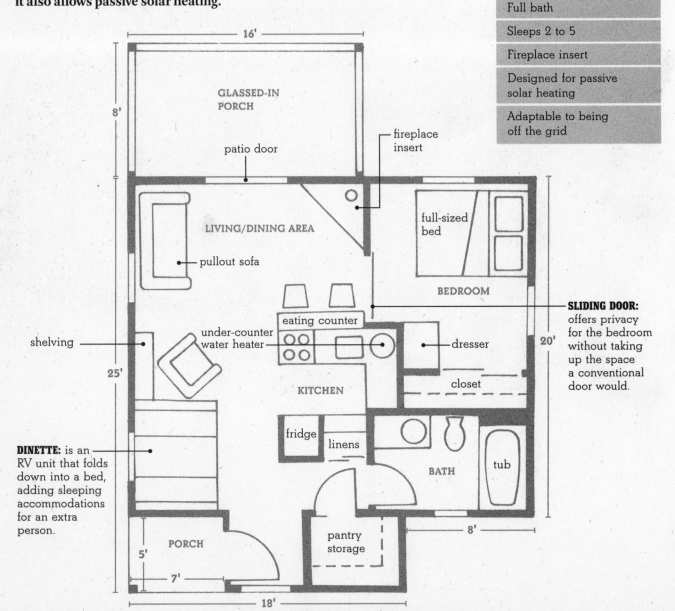

16'

8'

GLASSED-IN PORCH

patio door

fireplace insert

full-sized bed

LIVING/DINING AREA

BEDROOM

pullout sofa

SLIDING DOOR: offers privacy for the bedroom without taking up the space a conventional door would.

shelving

eating counter

under-counter water heater

dresser

closet

20'

25'

KITCHEN

fridge

linens

BATH

tub

DINETTE: is an RV unit that folds down into a bed, adding sleeping accommodations for an extra person.

PORCH

pantry storage

5'

7'

8'

18'

GLASSED-IN PORCH:
offers a great view
of the surrounding
environment from
the living area.

CLERESTORY WINDOWS:
bring light to the interior
and can be opened in
warm weather for natural
ventilation.

PITCHED ROOF: could
support solar panels if
oriented to the south.

FAMILY CABIN

The layout of this design is more like that of a small house than a cabin. It incorporates a full kitchen and bathroom, a great room with fireplace, and sleeping accommodations for up to six people in two private bedrooms and on a pullout sofa. Pocket doors in the bedrooms offer privacy without taking up valuable space.

Features
740 square feet
Full kitchen
Full bath
Sleeps 4 to 6
Fireplace
Adaptable to being off the grid

GREAT-ROOM FIREPLACE: acts as a heat sink, retaining heat and then releasing it back into the living space.

FULL-SIZED BEDS: could offer additional storage space with drawers or boxes underneath.

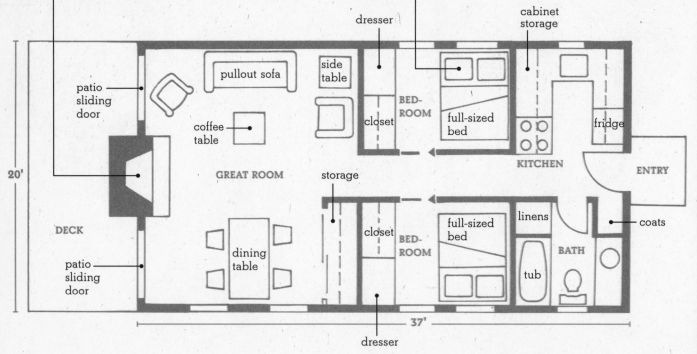

DECK: could easily be converted to an open or screened porch by extending the roof.

PATIO SLIDING DOORS: flank the fireplace; orienting these doors to the south would bring passive solar heating to the cabin.

PITCHED ROOF: could support solar panels if oriented to the south.

POCONO WOODS CABIN

The spacious living space makes this cabin comfortable for extended stays. At its center is a great room with a wood-burning stove, with open views out the adjacent glass doors. It also features a private sleeping floor complete with full bath.

Features

840 square feet

Full kitchen

One and a half baths

Sleeps 2 to 4

Adaptable to being off the grid

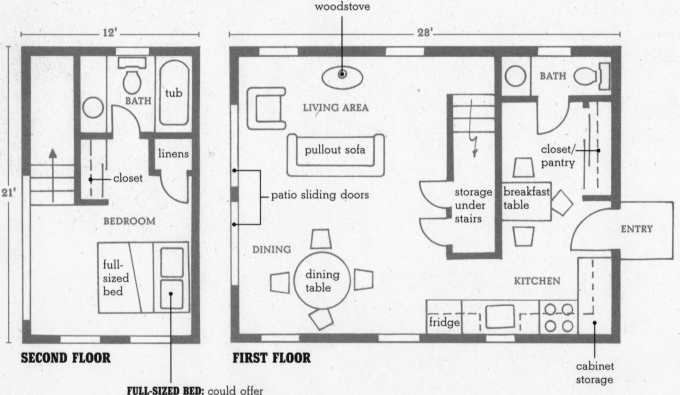

SECOND FLOOR

FIRST FLOOR

woodstove

12'

21'

28'

BATH

tub

linens

closet

BEDROOM

full-sized bed

LIVING AREA

pullout sofa

patio sliding doors

DINING

dining table

storage under stairs

breakfast table

BATH

closet/pantry

ENTRY

KITCHEN

fridge

cabinet storage

FULL-SIZED BED: could offer additional storage space with drawers or boxes underneath.

PITCHED ROOF: could support solar panels if either side is oriented to the south.

CLERESTORY WINDOWS: bring light to the interior and can be opened in warm weather for natural ventilation.

GREAT-ROOM END WALL: would be an ideal location for a deck, patio, or porch, overlooking the best view from the cabin.

PATIO SLIDING DOORS: open the main living space to the great outdoors.

DESIGN:

ARCHITECTURE,
LOGISTICS,
ENVIRONMENT

GOOD DESIGN IS ESSENTIAL FOR GOOD LIVING IN ANY SPACE, BUT IT IS ESPECIALLY IMPORTANT IN A SMALL SPACE.

In many contexts, the term *design* means the architecture of a structure or the layout of its furnishings. But good design is not limited to how a cabin looks. Instead, it considers every aspect of the building, from the foundation to the furnishings to the fuel supply. Because so many factors must be considered, the best approach is to allow a design to evolve over time. A good rule to follow is to design early, design often, and live with your ideas for a period of time before undertaking construction.

The side of my refrigerator faces into my dining/living room. I stick ideas I'm working with up on the refrigerator (on a cork bulletin board) and live with them for a while. Each time I pass by them, I react to them and often change arrangements. When I get a floor plan that has been up for several weeks without changes, I'm satisfied that it is the best solution.

In this chapter, you'll find a discussion on the concerns common to any small cabin design. Your particular design will have its own considerations, of course, depending on where you intend to build it, how you intend to build it, and how you intend to use it. Take the time to get familiar with every aspect of the design and building process. Live with ideas for a while. Visit the site often with your latest design ideas on paper. Talk to architects, builders, and contractors. Talk to friends or relatives who have cabins. Get the whole family in on the process. Start looking for services in the area of the cabin: excavators, building contractors, sewer and septic contractors, well drillers, cement contractors, building suppliers, plumbing suppliers, electricians, and so on. Start pricing materials and services to get an idea of the budget you will need. Ask a lot of questions.

NEED-BASED DESIGN

The term *need-based design* means, appropriately, design based on your specific needs. Need-based design tends to keep the overall size of a cabin to a minimum because it makes very clear what is essential and what is not. To begin, try answering the questions below:

How many people will the cabin need to accommodate? As the plans in this book show, even a small cabin can accommodate upward of 12 people if you design for that capacity from the start.

How long do you plan to stay at the cabin? If you intend to use it primarily for only a couple of days at a time, you may be happy with a galley kitchen with a dorm-sized refrigerator, a three-quarter bath, and minimal storage. If you plan to stay for a week or more at a time, you'll probably want a full refrigerator and possibly a freezer, along with a full bath and more storage for extra gear and clothing.

How do you intend to use the cabin? If it's a hunting cabin, you'll want a place to hang muddy or wet clothing and gear and possibly a secure gun rack. If it's an artist's retreat, you'll want space in which to work and storage for your materials of choice. And if it's a family vacation cabin, you may want designated kid-sized sleeping accommodations and play space for rainy days.

In what seasons will you use the cabin? If you intend to use it in colder weather, you'll need to provide for heat and insulation. In very hot weather you'll want to be sure to have good ventilation and airflow.

Will your needs change over time? Forethought and good design are a cabin builder's least expensive and most valuable resources. An empty-nest couple may dream of a small cabin in the woods, far away from their children. But nature has a way of adding to a family over time, and in time that same couple who wanted to be alone on weekends might not be able to bear being parted from their adorable grandchildren. With good planning, you can produce a small cabin that can be expanded over time to meet possible future needs. A full kitchen and bathroom in such a small cabin might seem unnecessary at first, but when three lovely grandchildren are bouncing around the place, those items are necessities. It is far less expensive to design and build the full

Ask, Ask, and Ask

A little tale: I have a friend with whom I travel occasionally. She has traveled all over the world for the past 20 years. We were recently in Japan. Eight cities and seven hotels in 15 days; not once were we lost or did we miss a travel connection. She did business and I saw a lot of art, architecture, and Japanese culture. I walked around those cities for most of every day. We used every form of transportation except rickshaw. Our secret was to ask a lot of questions — really, *a lot* of questions. Outside of Tokyo, very few people speak English. We spoke almost no Japanese. I find people everywhere in the world to be very helpful. So I politely asked, and they did their best to understand and answer my questions. The moral of this tale: Ask, ask, and ask!

Don't be afraid to ask questions of builders, contractors, and suppliers — no question is ever too dumb to ask. And don't be afraid to ask for help — most people are happy to share their expertise.

kitchen and bath for the original small cabin than to demolish an existing small kitchen and half bath in order to add full-sized ones later. (Building the cabin as a series of modules, as described in chapter 3, can allow the structure to grow as family needs change.)

LOCAL BUILDING CODES

Local ordinances are a controlling factor in cabin design. Cedar shakes for roofing and siding may not be allowed in areas prone to forest fires. Some areas demand that cabins be equipped with solid wood window shutters that can be closed and locked for security when the cabin's not in use. (There are areas where the local cottage industry is breaking into cabins in the off-season.) Some areas will allow outhouses, others demand composting toilets, yet others require a flush toilet with septic tank and drain field. Before you get too far along in your cabin design, be sure to check with your local building department to determine what, if any, local ordinances will apply to your construction. And, of course, you'll need to have your plans approved by the local building department before you commence construction.

AESTHETIC CONCERNS

Style is important in designing a cabin that you can be happy with over time. A cabin design translated into twig architecture has a very different aesthetic from the same cabin design done in chrome and stainless steel. Pink corrugated asphalt roofing imparts a distinct sense of style; cedar shakes impart a very different sense of style. A log cabin can bring out the "Lincoln-ness" in all of us. Here you are limited only by your personal taste.

Try to employ some very inexpensive ways to window-shop for aesthetic and design ideas. An afternoon at a local bookstore with a latte, looking over a handful of architecture and interior design magazines, can be a useful way to get ideas. Pack your digital camera and take a Sunday afternoon drive around your favorite lake or along a pleasant river, and it will reveal a number of beautiful cabins with design elements you might want to borrow. If you're lucky enough to see the owners, a little flattery will probably get you inside for pictures, too. Ask the owners what they like and don't like about their cabin and what they would change. Use photo-editing software to cut and paste features from one cabin photo to another, or start a scrapbook.

LOCATION

The topography of the building site dictates the design parameters of the cabin. For example, lakeside lots tend to be very narrow, and so most folks building on such lots want a cabin that is narrow but long. A cabin cantilevered out from a rocky outcrop on a mountain ridge demands a different kind of consideration. Areas prone to flooding or near the ocean dictate that cabins are built on stilts instead of foundations.

The local climate also influences design considerations. Warm climates allow for large windows and plenty of ventilation. In a tropical climate, only roofing and a few interior walls may be necessary. Cold climates demand smaller windows, thick insulation, and a source of heat. In warm weather, you may enjoy having a deck or a porch. Decks are wonderful in shady locales or when steady breezes are available, but those set in direct sun can bake you. A deep porch can protect a cabin's living space from the sun, but you'll need to site it appropriately so it doesn't block the sun from heating the cabin in colder winter weather.

Climate may also dictate your choice of building materials. In a hot, moist, tropical climate, masonry construction is necessary. In most climates, pressure-treated lumber is a necessity where wood comes in contact with surface soils.

ACCESS

The accessibility of your building site will affect two design considerations: the delivery of materials and the availability of basic utilities such as fuel, electricity, and water. If you're going to be ordering large quantities of building materials from a local lumberyard, for example, will the delivery truck be able to unload those materials directly at your site? If you're hoping to build modules off-site and trailer them in, will you be able to get a trailer to the site? If you need a crane to help place modules on the foundation, will it be able to get to the site and have room to maneuver?

Will your cabin be able to access a town water line, or do you need to arrange to have a well drilled or to capture rainwater in a cistern? If your building site is remote, electric power lines may not be readily accessible. If that's the case, is it more cost-efficient to pay the local electric company to extend its line to your site or to design an off-the-grid power system for your cabin?

Local Wildlife

If you take the time up front to consider the potential interactions between your cabin and local wildlife, you'll thank yourself later. A cabin located next to a 6,000-acre bog may need a well-screened porch to separate mosquitoes from people. In bear country, animal-proofing a cabin may be a necessity. A cabin I once owned suffered from porcupines; they gnawed on every inch of exposed wood not protected by an armor of small nails.

In some areas, insect damage to structures may be a problem. In warmer climates, for example, any wood in contact with the ground becomes a super-highway for insects to enter the structure. Cabins built in insect-prone areas need to be elevated off the ground on either piers or tall footers. Piers and footers keep the lumber of the cabin off the ground and also allow air circulation. Insects, mold, and mildew love dark, damp places. Elevating a cabin helps solve all of these problems.

You may decide you want your cabin to exist off the grid in either situation, which dictates important design considerations. For example, solar energy is intelligent design in some areas, while installing a portable generator makes more sense in other areas, and for a mountaintop cabin using a wind turbine to generate power may work best. In areas where firewood is plentiful, cheap cooking and heating with wood makes sense; in a desert area, propane may be the fuel of choice. See chapter 7 for more discussion on energy independence.

BUDGET

Budget is always an important consideration, and it dictates style factors, the size of the finished cabin, and the time it takes to build it. Do you have the funds to build the cabin all at once, or will you need to build it in stages? Building in stages is a good way to spread the costs over time, allowing you to pay out of pocket instead of financing the construction. Modular construction lends itself well to building in stages; see chapter 3 for more details.

The materials you choose will, of course, be determined by your budget. T-111 plywood sheeting is inexpensive, but it does have a certain look. Masonry walls built of local river rock impart another look, though they can cost a fortune to build — unless you build them yourself, in which case you may be at it for months.

Amenities are usually a budgetary consideration. Grilling dinner on a small portable gas grill is certainly less expensive, if also less romantic, than grilling over a large fieldstone fireplace. The number and size of windows is a light and ventilation consideration, but it is also a budgetary consideration.

Designing a budget starts with the question: "What do I have to spend?" Whether you have cash on hand or will be taking out a loan, do the math so that you know exactly how much you can afford. And be sure to factor in at least a 10 percent overrun on your estimated costs, so that you're not caught short at the end of the project.

Item number one of the budget is the cost of the building lot. Site preparation needs attention, too; if you must clear land for your cabin site or driveway, that expense must be factored in.

We can now turn our attention to the cabin itself. Once the design phase is complete, you will "cost out" your cabin, that is, determine how much it will cost to build. An architect or builder will be able to provide fairly accurate estimates of cost. If you're working on your own, start at the foundation and work your way up. Here is a list of areas to consider:

➤ Foundation work

➤ Framing

➤ Siding

➤ Roofing

➤ Interior drywall

➤ Interior trim

➤ Electrical, including electrical service to the cabin

➤ Plumbing: water and sewer

➤ Cabinetry

➤ Appliances and fixtures

➤ Heating

➤ Special features, such as solar-electric and hot water systems

➤ Backfilling, grading, and landscaping

It may seem like an overwhelming task, but take one area at a time and price it out.

Of course, builders and architects will do all of this for you, for a fee. Many soon-to-be cabin owners would consider that well worth the money. But for those who would prefer to do at least some of the work themselves, the cost savings can be considerable. I just completed a new kitchen for a little more than one-quarter of what a kitchen/bath company would have charged me. I did the design work and labor myself. I bought the appliances, transported them, and installed them. I laid the hardwood floors, tiled the backsplashes, and did the electrical work, too. I shopped hard for good materials at a good price. It cost me $4,300 for a kitchen that was quoted, by a local builder, for "ballpark $15,000."

The Three-Season Cabin for All Seasons

If you're thinking of building a three-season cabin but might possibly have use for it in the coldest months, consider building an interior cube, engineered with a very high R value, to house plumbing, water, and utilities. This interior utility cube could be kept above freezing at a fraction of the cost of heating a whole cabin, providing hot and cold running water and unfrozen sewer pipes year-round. With these utilities available on demand all year, you wouldn't have to winterize the cabin by draining the water system, and your three-season cabin can be used in all four seasons.

SCHEDULE

The ideal way to build a cabin is all at one time. You would flip open your cell phone and call a local architect and have him design and build your dream cabin. The architect would in turn hire the contractor, who might hire subcontractors, and they would all work together to get the job done.

"Once and done" is a good philosophy, but budget and time concerns may not make this possible. Cutting out all of these middlemen would save money, but doing it on your own takes time.

A smart way to design a cabin is to build in stages, working within the limitations of your available time and financial resources to, over time, get the cabin you want. A basic cabin can be enjoyed as a retreat and also provide living space while additions are being made to enlarge its design. For example: A small starter cabin may be 12 feet by 12 feet, or 144 square feet. A cabin this size can be built by the owner in one season. The second season, 8-foot-by-12-foot porches can be added to opposing ends of the cabin. These porches can be used for leisure, sleeping, eating, or outdoor cooking. At some future time, those porches can be enclosed and incorporated into living space. One can become the kitchen/dining area and the other a master bedroom. The next season, two porches added on the unused sides of the cabin can stay as porches, or become sleeping porches (if well screened), or be enclosed and converted into additional bedrooms. The original 144-square-foot cabin would then revert to a common living area. This cabin design project can, over a three-year implementation schedule, become a 528-square-foot cabin with three bedrooms.

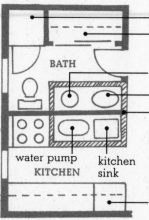

shower
closet
BATH
under-counter water heater
bathroom sink
heavily insulated counter and base with small electric baseboard heating unit with thermostat inside
water pump
KITCHEN
kitchen sink
fridge

A cabin owner does not need to keep the entire living space heated in order to prevent the plumbing from freezing. With just a little heat from an electric baseboard unit, a through-the-wall insulated cube can keep the water heater, water pump, and sink drains from freezing. The shower and toilet should be plumbed with low-point water drains, and when the cabin is not in use the shower drain and toilet should be treated with RV antifreeze (which is nontoxic).

CONSTRUCTION MATERIALS

The materials you choose play the determining role in your cabin's cost, quality, and style. Here is where building small has great advantage: limiting the overall size of your cabin allows you to dedicate your money to building with quality materials that will serve you well over time.

I use local materials whenever possible, both because it's the ecological thing to do (saving transportation fuel and stimulating the local economy) and because it makes sense aesthetically. Rough-sawn barnwood siding makes sense in northern forests; adobe makes sense in the American Southwest. Chefs talk about the advantages of preparing dishes using local ingredients and pairing them with local wines. The same can be said about building.

The use of recycled or remanufactured material may make a lot of sense if you live in an area where older housing or industrial structures are being either torn down or replaced with new housing. You may even be lucky enough to find a local business that specializes in used windows, doors, moldings, trim, lumber, brick, and so on. See chapter 5 for more details.

Using premanufactured components, such as whole-house modules, panels, or roof trusses, may make sense if you want to build quickly or don't intend to do much of the construction work yourself. See chapter 4 for more details.

CONSTRUCTION METHOD

No single construction method is best. The design of the cabin, the complexity of that design, and the accessibility of the building site are all important factors in choosing a construction method. Take the time to sit down and cost out the building of your cabin in a number of ways. Consult builders or an architect, or do a lot of homework yourself.

Stick-Built

The term *stick-built* refers to buildings constructed on-site from dimensional lumber. This term usually differentiates buildings constructed one piece at a time from buildings constructed with panels or modules. There is ongoing debate in the construction industry as to which method is best for constructing houses. Perhaps the best perspective is that no one method is better than the other. I've found that the best method often differs from project to project, depending on site, schedule, and budget.

With its centuries-old building style, the post-and-beam cabin has a classic character. Traditionally the heavy beams remain exposed in the interior.

Post and Beam

Post-and-beam construction is an old idea that has regained traction. Most Colonial and nineteenth-century barns were built using this method. In modern house construction, the house is supported with a heavy framework of beams (timbers) that remain exposed to the interior of the house. The charm of this method is that the beams, and their character, remain visible. Sheathing, insulation, and siding are applied on the outside of the timber framework to complete the house.

Log Cabins

The log cabin is part of the romance Americans have with the past. In pioneer days, trees were felled, hauled to the building site, and notched to fit tightly together. The walls were stacks of logs piled one on top of the other. Any voids between the logs were chinked with whatever material was readily available to keep the weather out.

Log cabins evoke a sense of the pioneering spirit. They can be built by hand the old-fashioned way, but kits make the job easier and faster.

Modern log construction is usually done from a kit. Logs are carefully prepared, cut to size, and notched in a factory, then shipped to the home site as a kit. Kit log homes go together on the site relatively quickly, since much of the labor took place in the factory. Log cabin kits may seem expensive, but they need no other sheeting or insulation. This consideration makes them competitive with conventional construction methods. Assembling a cabin from a log kit might be an exciting and cost-saving building method. If the romance of a log cabin appeals to you, a log cabin kit may be an excellent choice.

Straw Bale

Straw bale is another construction method of pioneer days that is regaining popularity. Straw bale construction usually starts with a foundation slab. A simple framework is erected to help support the straw bales and the roof. The walls are then constructed from tightly packed bales of straw, with the bales set much like giant cement blocks. Electrical wiring and reinforcing wire lattices may be placed between the layers of straw bales. The straw bales are then plastered over with a layer of masonry stucco to protect the straw from the elements. Straw bale cabins usually have a large roof overhang to protect the walls from exposure to the elements. (Straw may not be a good choice in climates where dampness is an issue.)

Straw bale construction yields well-insulated, natural-looking homes. One of their best attributes is ease of construction: any reasonably handy person can put one up.

reinforcing bars hold straw bales in place

Straw bale cabins tend to have an organic feeling, in the same way adobe buildings appear organic and sculptural. Straw bale construction lends itself to owner building, but it is labor-intensive. If sweat equity is your goal, this might be the construction method for you.

Pole Building

Pole buildings offer some exciting opportunities to the small cabin builder. They are relatively inexpensive to build and offer unobstructed interior space. Because of the truss system they utilize in their roofing systems, they need no interior support. The trusses can be custom-engineered for nearly any width up to about 36 feet, and all that is open interior space.

Pole construction usually employs poles set 8 feet on center, with the trusses attached to those uprights. Horizontal lumber, known as purling, connects the poles. This layout suggests that 8 feet would be a likely module to design on: a building of two modules would be 16 feet in length, three modules would be 24 feet, and so on.

Pole buildings can be very energy efficient. The uprights are usually 6×6 or 8×8 posts, so they produce thick walls that can be well insulated. The flooring of a pole building could be a poured concrete slab with a radiant heating system cast into it, which is a very efficient way to heat a structure.

purling

Because pole construction is designed to be free span, it gives cabin owners great flexibility in how to use the interior space. Sliding walls and panels work well in pole cabins; they can be opened or closed as needed to open or divide spaces.

uprights are widely spaced

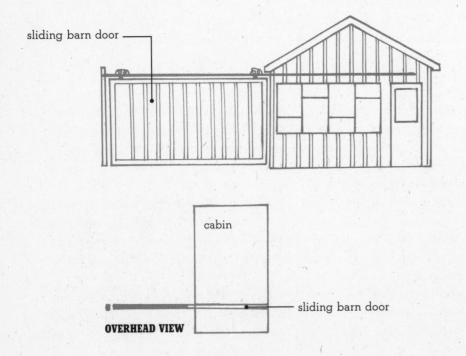

sliding barn door

cabin

sliding barn door

OVERHEAD VIEW

End walls could be nearly all glass and entrance doors. A set of sliding barn doors, installed outside the end walls, could be closed and locked for security when the cabin is not in use or in severe weather.

Pole building manufacturers generally design their buildings to work in farm or industrial settings. Since such buildings will never win an award for aesthetics, a pole-built horse barn might be more aesthetically pleasing. Manufacturers design these barns with standard poles and trusses but usually give them cladding (siding) that better fits the aesthetics of domestic architecture — in a word, socially acceptable pole building.

Masonry

One of the oldest and most reliable construction methods is masonry construction. Stone, brick, cement block, and even glass bottles and aluminum cans can be incorporated into cabin walls and held together with mortar. Masonry cabins tend to be impervious to the weather and very long-lasting.

Constructing a masonry cabin is labor intensive; as with straw bale, sweat equity can be a factor. The materials tend to be more expensive than conventional building materials, but if you have a good local source for materials, it might be the building method of choice.

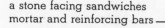

a stone facing sandwiches mortar and reinforcing bars

Cabins built of stone, brick, or other masonry materials have a strong sense of heft and timelessness. Almost nothing is prettier than a small stone cabin built of the same rock that surrounds it.

Metal Buildings

I grew up right after World War II when military surplus Quonset huts were common. They were cheap and easy to transport and erect without special equipment. Two men could set one up within a week. They were put to a variety of uses, from homes to body shops, storage buildings, retail stores, beer distributors, and so on.

You might think a metal hut would be too hot during warm weather and too cold in cold weather, but during World War II, Quonset huts were used throughout the Pacific and Alaska to house just about all the Army's, Navy's, and Air Force's personnel. The military developed insulation packages so that the huts could house soldiers in reasonable comfort. Today, spray-on insulation made from recycled newspaper and a fire retardant is ideal for the curved surface of a Quonset hut.

Quonset huts and Quonset-style metal buildings are still available. The curved walls create a design challenge, but they lend themselves to a variety of applications and cabin building. The huts are usually built on a concrete slab. Depending on the climate, a footer may be necessary. Utilities are usually put in place and the floor slab poured over them.

Depending on materials selection, the curved walls of Quonset-style huts can give a cabin an earthy, sheltered feeling or a modern, high-tech character.

Adapting Garage Designs

Pole and post-and-beam barn builders usually have a variety of garage designs that could be easily adapted for small cabins. Some offer carriage houses that have second floors designed to accommodate apartments. This configuration would leave the first floor for parking and storage of vehicles, boats, trailers, or other toys. It would be a comforting thought to have your fishing boat and its trailer or your ATV stored in a secure place. In addition, second-floor living space provides a better view and improved natural ventilation and is generally more secure than ground-level living.

Hybrids

Many cabin designers mix and match building methods to their ideas. Pole-barn methods are merged with post-and-beam construction methods. Stick building is combined with manufactured panels. For example, the classic Adirondack cabin is fieldstone on the first floor and frame construction above. A premanufactured ranch house may be placed on top of a first floor made of cement blocks to create the classic "Poconos raised rancher." Generally a good rule to follow is that the construction method is dictated by design ideas. Arrive at a design you love and then select the building method that will best allow you to build it. And always, always keep an eye out for local materials and resources.

FOUNDATIONS

Though you may never see much of it, your cabin's foundation — a full foundation, a concrete slab, or piers — as a base upon which to build is an important consideration. Topography, climate, and seasonal use tend to dictate the type of foundation selected. Full foundations with cellars or crawl spaces may be necessary for cabins that will be used extensively in the winter to provide additional space for water pumps, furnaces, or heaters. Crawl spaces and cellars also provide storage space.

A concrete slab may be the simplest solution for a foundation. Footers are usually dug and poured first. Also known as footings, footers are concrete bases that support and distribute the weight of walls or piers. Footers are necessary to protect foundation slabs from heaving in cold climates; they're usually placed deep enough to be immune to seasonal ground freezing. Utilities such as water, plumbing, and electricity (including radiant heating, solar hot water, or conventional hot water tubing or coils) are put in place and the slab is poured over them. Concrete floors meant as part of a passive solar heating system (see chapter 7) should be dark in color. A number of textured and patterned surfaces can be pressed into the floor before the concrete cures; the floor can be textured and colored to look like dark flagstone or brick.

In damp building conditions or places where flooding is likely, placing cabins on piers may be the best solution. Cabins raised on piers can provide storage space or even a parking area below.

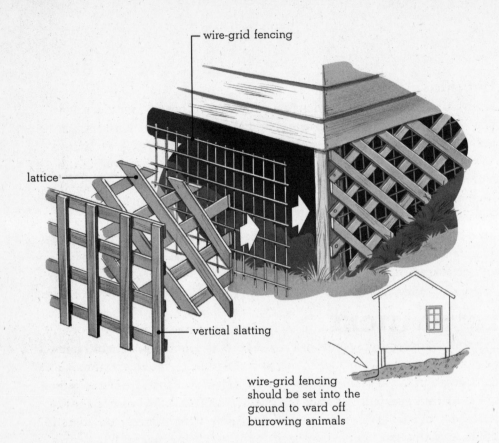

wire-grid fencing

lattice

vertical slatting

wire-grid fencing should be set into the ground to ward off burrowing animals

Wire-grid fencing prevents animals from getting into crawl spaces and under decks and porches; woodwork, lattice, or vertical slatting can conceal the fencing.

Good ventilation is important for crawl spaces and under decks and porches, as moisture buildup will shorten the life of lumber and provide a place for mold and mildew to grow. Proper ventilation usually entails placing vents that open to the prevailing breezes on one side of the cabin and a second set of vents on the opposite side of the space to encourage a cross breeze.

Unwelcome Visitors

Crawl spaces and cellars are favorite places for wild critters to take up residence. Squirrels, chipmunks, raccoons, skunks, groundhogs, and snakes can make these spaces home. It is impossible to tell a skunk to politely go away! Even bears have been known to hibernate under cabins, decks, or porches.

Wire fencing or hardware cloth set a foot or so deep into the ground around the perimeter of a crawl space, porch, or deck will discourage wild things from claiming those spaces as home. Lattice or vertical slatting placed over the wire will hide it and add another barrier layer.

MAKING THE MOST OF SMALL SPACES

Small cabins are small because they have a small footprint. Though cabins may have a small footprint, with good design, they can offer a comfortable living space. The challenge is to create that feeling of space in a small cabin. I find that, in particular, high ceilings and strategically placed windows make even very small cabins feel comfortable.

High Ceilings

High ceilings give a sense of roominess and space in even a small footprint. They also let in more light and make ventilation easier. And increasing ceiling height yields space with less expense than adding floor space.

The additional ceiling height can be used for storage. (After all, small cabins, by definition, have small storage spaces.) For example, two rows of cabinets could be hung in the kitchen, one over the other, doubling the kitchen storage. A small folding kitchen stool provides access to the higher set of cabinets. In the bedroom, additional shelving could be mounted on the walls; using clear plastic storage tubs on this shelving would add visible, climate- and insect-proof storage. In the living room, a kayak or canoe could be stored by hanging it from the ceiling with a pulley system. That same pulley system could double as a wash line to dry wet clothing on rainy days.

One drawback with high ceilings is that warm air rises and collects near the peak of the roof during the heating season. Installing a simple auxiliary duct system can overcome this problem. Install a duct with an air intake near the high point of the cabin roof and extending down to near the floor. Equip that duct with a small circulation fan that is reversible. In the winter, the fan is set to draw warm air from near the ceiling and recirculate it to the floor. In the summer the fan is set to reverse the airflow, drawing cool air from near the floor and circulating it near the roof. Install a thermostat near the top end of the duct and airflow will be changed automatically.

Window Placement

Strategically placed windows open up living spaces. Windows can be positioned to take advantage of a good view or to hide a bad view. In the 1950s, the hot design idea was the picture window — a large window designed to be the focal point of the living or dining room. The implication was that the view through the window was a work of art. This idea is not a bad one to keep in mind. If a view of the beach when you get out of bed in the morning is important to you, then a window placed to take advantage of this view is appropriate.

If your cabin is in the woods, on the beach, or lakeside, it's nice to be able to see your surroundings from inside. Windows bring the outside in, establishing a link to the environment. Windows in primary living spaces are more important than those in lesser spaces. Windows in halls and entrance foyers, for example, are not as important as windows in living, dining, and sleeping spaces. The bathroom is an exception to this general rule: natural ventilation is a necessity in bathrooms.

Window placement also plays a key role in cross ventilation and passive heating. Good natural ventilation can greatly reduce the need for fans, which in turn reduces your electrical needs. Generally, this means having windows and doors situated across from each other to promote the flow of air; you may, for example, want windows in the southwest and the northeast if the prevailing winds are in that direction. As a general rule, north-facing windows are of little advantage: little light and little access to prevailing airflow are available from the north, and winter's cold blast is usually from that direction as well. South-facing windows, on the other hand, are an important factor in passive solar heating, as the sun's rays will hit them directly in wintertime, helping to heat the cabin.

Lofts

Lofts adapt well to high ceiling heights and are useful as sleeping spaces. Lofts increase living space without increasing the footprint of the cabin. As an additional benefit, lofts and second floors cost less per square foot than the same space on a single floor.

Safe access to a loft is a necessity. Ladders, library ladders, ship's ladders, spiral staircases, and steep steps are the usual accesses to loft spaces. Good handrails are a must for stairs, as are safety rails at the edge of lofts. If privacy is an issue, you may want to attach a canvas panel to the loft rails, or you may dispense with rails entirely in favor of half walls.

At its simplest, a loft is a sleeping nook tucked under the roof. In bigger buildings lofts can feature multiple rooms, bathrooms, reading areas, and more.

Sliding Screens and Doors

Much of the architecture in Japan deals with small spaces, and one design element I saw a lot of there was the shoji screen, a paper screen serving as a sliding wall or partition. Shoji screens have been a part of Japanese architecture for many centuries. The oldest Shinto shrine in Japan, located where the Tone River empties into the Pacific Ocean, utilizes shoji screens. Nowadays shoji screens are used in everything from domestic housing and apartments to restaurants and hotel rooms.

In a small space, shoji-like sliding walls or screens are ideal. They allow you to divide off a sleeping area from the living space at night and then slide back the screens to maximize living space during the day. Also consider sliding doors or pocket doors for any doorways, interior or exterior. Since they don't have a swing, or radius of opening, they take up little space. A wall of patio sliding doors could be an integral part of a passive solar heating system. Those same patio doors could be opened in hot weather for natural air conditioning.

A sliding screen can separate a sleeping alcove from the main living space at night. During the day the alcove remains open, maximizing the cabin's living space.

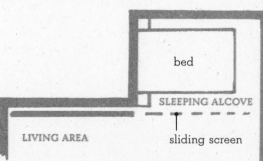

RV Innovations

Anyone beginning to design a small cabin should take a look at recreational vehicles (RVs) and travel trailers. This industry introduces an endless array of small-space design features each year. The competitive design race among RV and trailer manufacturers is fueling a great amount of innovation, and these inventive ideas can benefit your small cabin design. Recreational vehicle shows and dealers are good places to see a variety of models with a wide range of equipment available. Look at the different brands and sizes. See how they use space and place appliances. You'll find simple yet practical ideas, such as:

➡ Queen-sized beds that lift up to provide storage space under them

➡ Beds with a small triangle of mattress removed from the foot to better allow traffic past in a small bedroom

➡ Additional storage space made available by adding shelving over the head of the bed

➡ Wall cabinets placed high against the ceiling to allow bedroom access but increase storage

➡ Bunk-sized beds mounted on the wall over a full-sized bed that fold down for additional sleeping space or up for more living space

➡ Flat-screen televisions mounted into a shallow niche in the wall so as not to protrude into the room

➡ Automotive-type stereo equipment and speakers flush-mounted in a nightstand and speakers recessed into wall

I have spent the greater part of my life building and refurbishing cabins, houses, cottages, and other structures. Nothing has ever been done the same way twice. Your skills get better as you build. You learn new things. Building materials change. Building methods change. Local building codes change. It has been an evolutionary process. Learning new things has kept building interesting. Sharing what I have learned with others has also been rewarding. I hate to get Zen on you here, but the journey is as important as the destination. So take the time to design, and design again, and again. As your design evolves, so will you and your quest for the perfect compact cabin.

Building Yourself Versus Hiring Out

Will you build yourself or hire contractors? Which is most efficient and cost-effective? The answer lies mainly in your building skills. If you have the skills and training, doing the work yourself is both less expensive and more satisfying. Hiring out the work to professionals will make the work proceed more quickly, but it will cost more. I find a mix of the two is the best way for me to build.

If you're interested in acquiring more construction skills in order to do some of the work yourself, check with your local school district. Most districts have vocational technical schools, and many of those schools offer classes in carpentry, plumbing, electrical wiring, and so on. The large building supply chain stores also offer "how to do it" classes.

Any bed can be designed so that it doubles as a storage unit. With good hinges and supports or pulleys, the frame easily lifts up to provide access to storage underneath.

CUTAWAY CORNER: in a small bedroom, removing a corner from the bed makes it easy to enter the room without banging your shin.

A Murphy bed, as it's sometimes called, can be folded up against the wall during the day, maximizing floor space.

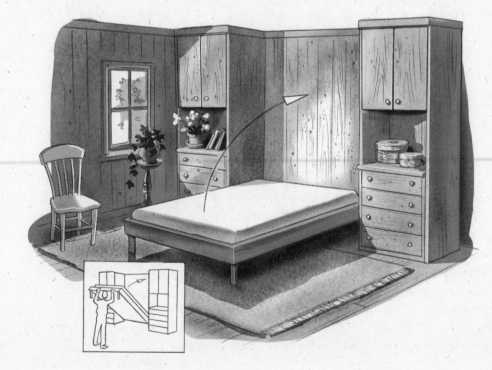

A MODULAR APPROACH TO CABIN DESIGN

A NOVEL APPROACH TO SMALL CABIN DESIGN IS THAT OF MODULARIZATION. A MODULE IS A BASIC UNIT THAT CAN BE EITHER REPEATED OR MODIFIED TO SUIT THE NEEDS OF THE CABIN DESIGNER.

Several advantages are found in this approach:

➤ A builder can start with a basic module and add modules as need and finances permit.

➤ Modules allow a designer to mix and match elements to best meet the needs of the cabin owner.

➤ Modules can be arranged in a great number of floor plans.

➤ Modules allow cabins to be designed to efficiently fit specific terrains.

➤ Modules allow cabins to be designed to accommodate groups of various sizes, from personal-sized cabins to large hunting or fishing camps. Using modules, a personal cabin could grow into a fishing or hunting camp.

➤ A modular approach allows a cabin to evolve as the owner lives in it or as family needs change. Cabins can grow bigger or smaller as needs dictate.

➤ Modules lend themselves well to premanufacturing, and the preassembled parts are easy to transport.

MIX-AND-MATCH MODULES

You'll find here modules for bedrooms, bathrooms, kitchens, living spaces, and decks and porches in a number of different configurations. They are designed to accommodate different numbers of people and a variety of needs and lifestyles. Each module is 12 feet by 12 feet, or 144 square feet. The modules may be strung together to produce a variety of cabin sizes, as seen below.

The modular system offered here allows for a great deal of flexibility in design. Using ¼-inch-to-the-foot ruled graph paper and a drawing pencil, you can do your own designing. Draw the modules you are interested in on the graph paper, and cut them out. They can then be arranged and rearranged until you arrive at the best combination for your needs.

Premanufacturing

Premanufacturing — that is, building sections off-site and transporting them to the building site as they're ready for installation — can greatly condense the time between the inception of design and the production of the finished cabin.

Preassembled modules of the size I suggest (12 feet by 12 feet) can be transported by trailer in the same way as modular housing. One idea is to purchase a trailer frame that is used under modular homes. The winter can be spent building the cabin (or partially building it) on the frame, and after the foundation work is done in the spring, the cabin sections can be moved to the site and installed. (A modular home dealer can do that job.)

Once the cabin is installed, the trailer wheels and axles are removed and the towing tongue is trimmed with a cutting torch. Skirting or siding then covers any hint that a trailer frame rests under the cabin.

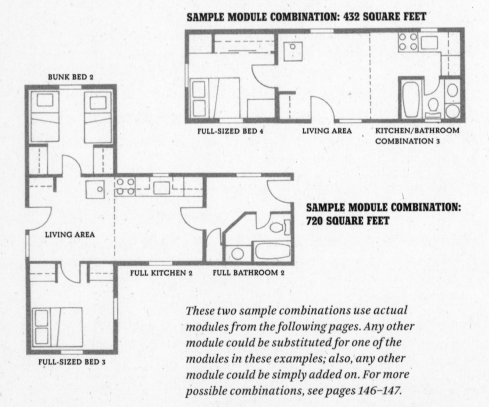

SAMPLE MODULE COMBINATION: 432 SQUARE FEET

FULL-SIZED BED 4   LIVING AREA   KITCHEN/BATHROOM COMBINATION 3

BUNK BED 2

LIVING AREA

FULL KITCHEN 2   FULL BATHROOM 2

FULL-SIZED BED 3

SAMPLE MODULE COMBINATION: 720 SQUARE FEET

These two sample combinations use actual modules from the following pages. Any other module could be substituted for one of the modules in these examples; also, any other module could be simply added on. For more possible combinations, see pages 146–147.

The following plans are offered as a starting point for the cabin designer. The ideas offered might inspire new ideas that suit the needs of the cabin designer better.

KITCHEN MODULES

These full kitchen modules offer full-sized refrigerators and stovetops, as well as plenty of counter and storage space.

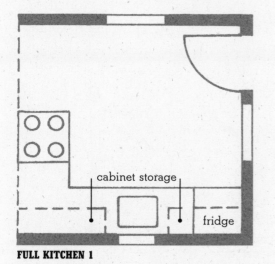

cabinet storage

fridge

FULL KITCHEN 1

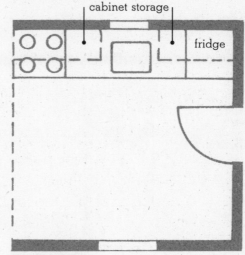

cabinet storage

fridge

FULL KITCHEN 2

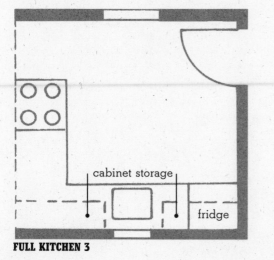

cabinet storage

fridge

FULL KITCHEN 3

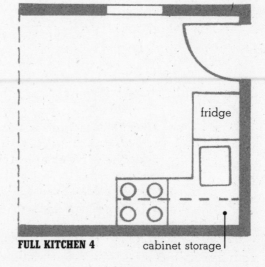

fridge

FULL KITCHEN 4

cabinet storage

BATHROOM MODULES

These larger bathroom modules accommodate a tub or shower and storage closets, either in or adjacent to the bathroom.

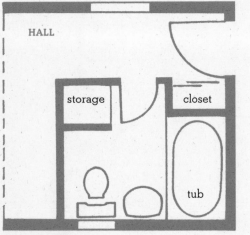

FULL BATHROOM 1

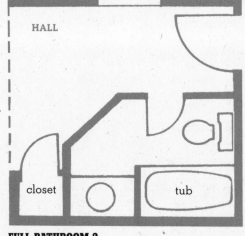

FULL BATHROOM 2

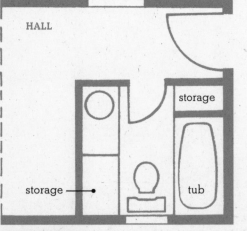

FULL BATHROOM 3

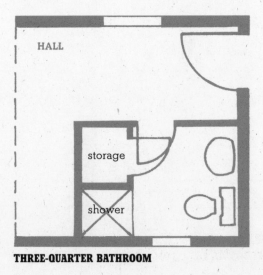

THREE-QUARTER BATHROOM

KITCHEN/BATHROOM COMBINATION MODULES

Modules that combine the kitchen and bathroom make very efficient use of space. Keeping all plumbing confined to a single module can make winterizing the cabin easier; a single module, rather than the entire cabin, can be kept heated just enough to keep the water lines from freezing.

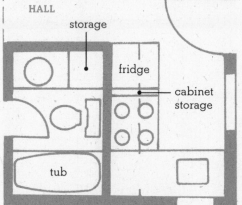
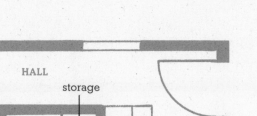

1: FULL KITCHEN/FULL BATHROOM

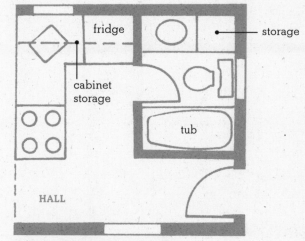

2: FULL KITCHEN/FULL BATHROOM

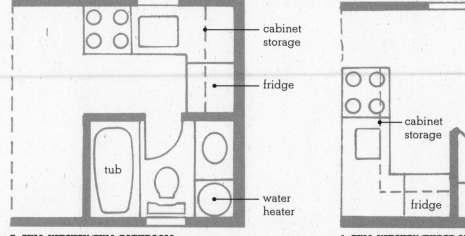

3: FULL KITCHEN/FULL BATHROOM

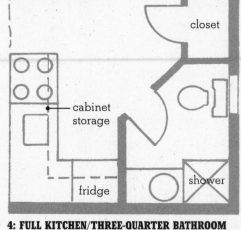

4: FULL KITCHEN/THREE-QUARTER BATHROOM

KITCHEN/BATHROOM COMBINATION MODULES (CONTINUED)

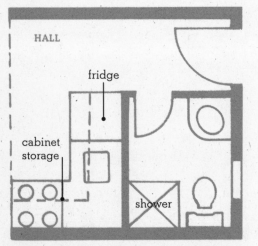

5: FULL KITCHEN/THREE-QUARTER BATHROOM

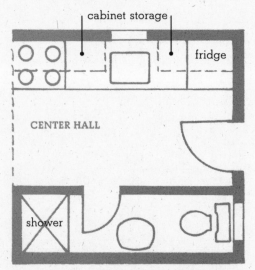

6: FULL KITCHEN/THREE-QUARTER BATHROOM

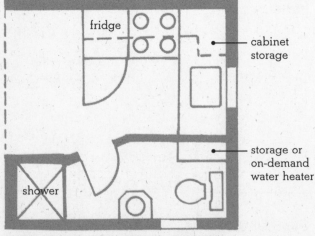

7: FULL KITCHEN/THREE-QUARTER BATHROOM

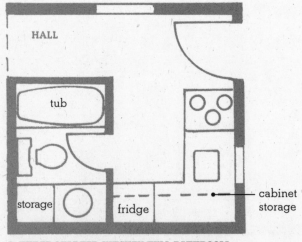

8: THREE-QUARTER KITCHEN/FULL BATHROOM

KITCHEN/BATHROOM
COMBINATION MODULES (CONTINUED)

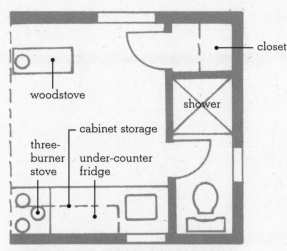

9: THREE-QUARTER KITCHEN/HALF BATHROOM

closet

shower

woodstove

three-burner stove

cabinet storage

under-counter fridge

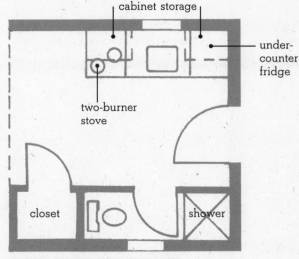

10: HALF KITCHEN/HALF BATHROOM

cabinet storage

under-counter fridge

two-burner stove

closet

shower

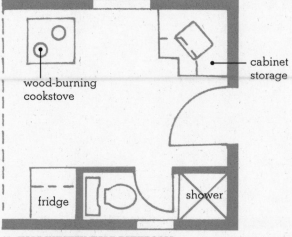

11: HALF KITCHEN/HALF BATHROOM

cabinet storage

wood-burning cookstove

fridge

shower

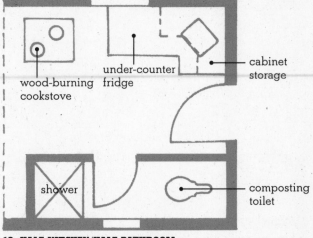

12: HALF KITCHEN/HALF BATHROOM

cabinet storage

under-counter fridge

wood-burning cookstove

shower

composting toilet

BEDROOM MODULES

Bedrooms can be either roomy affairs with plenty of open space or compact arrangements making efficient use of space. Bed sizes will, of course, be determined by the size and number of occupants expected to spend nights in the cabin.

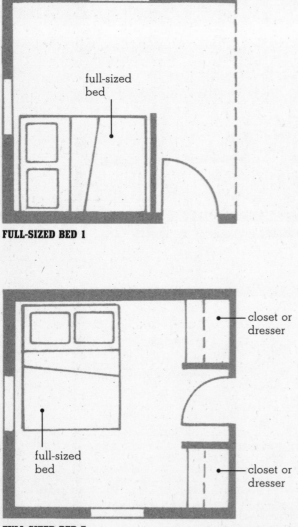

full-sized bed

FULL-SIZED BED 1

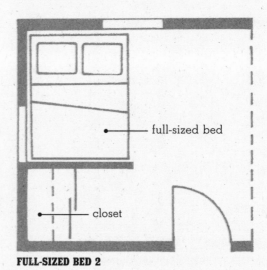

full-sized bed

closet

FULL-SIZED BED 2

closet or dresser

full-sized bed

closet or dresser

FULL-SIZED BED 3

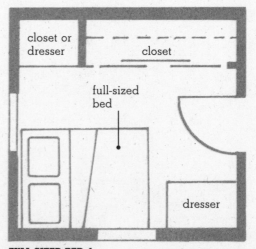

closet or dresser

closet

full-sized bed

dresser

FULL-SIZED BED 4

BEDROOM MODULES (CONTINUED)

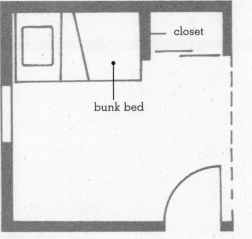

closet

bunk bed

BUNK BED 1

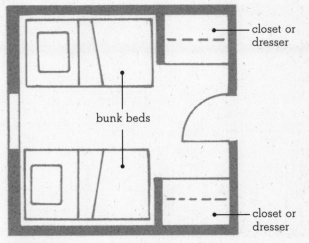

closet or dresser

bunk beds

closet or dresser

BUNK BED 2

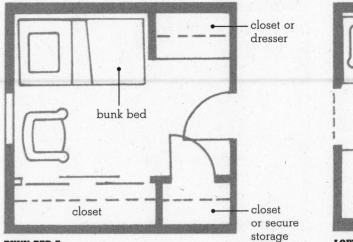

closet or dresser

bunk bed

closet

closet or secure storage

BUNK BED 3

chair below

storage

ladders

loft bed above

storage

LOFT BEDS

BEDROOM COMBINATION MODULES

If you think of your cabin's bed as just a place to lay your head, these combination modules may be just right for your design, folding beds into other spaces to make the most of cabin floor space.

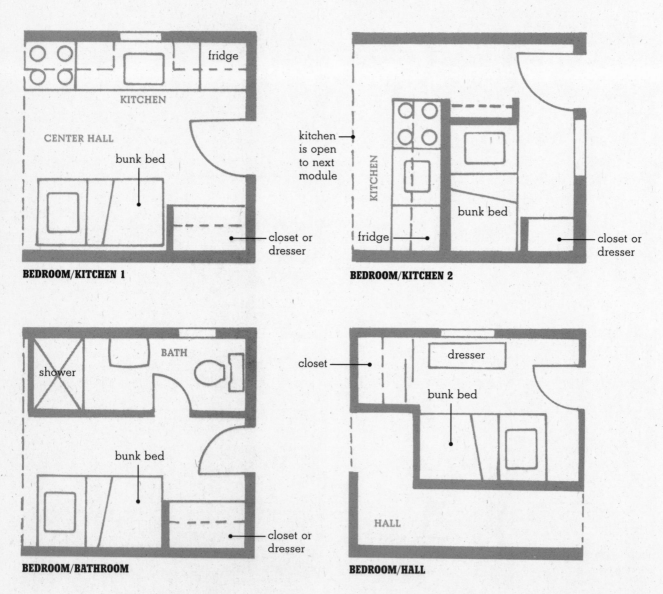

BEDROOM/KITCHEN 1

KITCHEN

CENTER HALL

bunk bed

closet or dresser

BEDROOM/KITCHEN 2

fridge

KITCHEN

kitchen is open to next module

bunk bed

closet or dresser

BEDROOM/BATHROOM

shower

BATH

bunk bed

closet or dresser

BEDROOM/HALL

closet

dresser

bunk bed

HALL

BEDROOM FEATURES

shelf overhead

storage underneath

In a bedroom module, a full-sized bed offers storage space both overhead and underneath.

storage

Bunk beds are perhaps best suited for children, but they offer compact sleeping arrangements and even storage beneath.

A bedroom storage space can accommodate both a hanging rod and a dresser.

A loft-style arrangement offers sleeping space, a cozy nook for reading, and storage.

loft bed

plenty of storage

LIVING-AREA MODULE

This is a basic living-area module with a woodstove. It could easily be restructured to fit with just about any combination of modules.

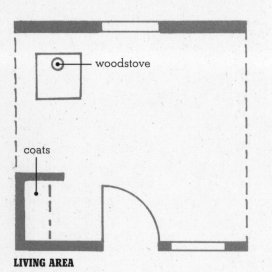

LIVING AREA

PORCH/DECK MODULES

A porch or deck can be tacked on to any outside wall.

DECK

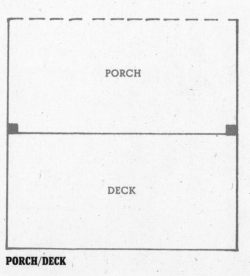

PORCH/DECK

CAMP MODULES

For a hunting camp, fishing camp, or other cabin intended to house a large number of people, you'll need a larger kitchen and more toilets.

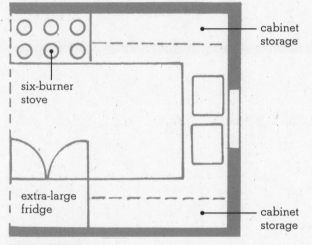

cabinet storage

six-burner stove

extra-large fridge

cabinet storage

CAMP KITCHEN

storage

toilet   toilet

double sink

shower   shower

CAMP BATHROOM

SAMPLE MODULE COMBINATIONS

Basing cabin design on 12-foot-by-12-foot modules allows the owner a great deal of creative flexibility. The modules can be strung together in whatever way best suits the owner's current and future needs.

K = *kitchen/bath combination*

L = *living area*

BED = *bedroom sleeping two*

BUNK = *bedroom with two bunk beds, sleeping four*

D = *deck*

CB = *camp bathroom*

CK = *camp kitchen*

576
square
feet

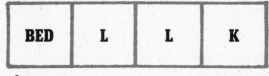

| BED | L | L | K |

sleeps 2

720
square
feet

	BUNK		
BED	L	L	K
	D		

sleeps 6

720
square
feet

			BUNK
BED	L	K (w/ hall)	L
	D		

sleeps 6

432
square
feet

BED	L	K

sleeps 2

576
square
feet

BED	BUNK (w/ hall)	L	K

sleeps 6

576
square
feet

BED	L	K	BED
	D		

sleeps 4

576
square
feet

	BUNK	
BED	L	K
	D	

sleeps 6

720
square
feet

		BED	
BED	BUNK (w/ hall)	L	K

sleeps 8

1,008
square
feet

			BUNK		
CB	BUNK (w/ hall)	BUNK (w/ hall)	L	L	CK

sleeps 12

USING MANUFACTURED STRUCTURAL COMPONENTS

ONE SERIOUS CONSIDERATION IN SMALL CABIN CONSTRUCTION IS UTILIZING MANUFACTURED COMPONENTS SUCH AS PANELS AND MODULAR BUILDING UNITS THAT ARE MADE OFF-SITE. MODULAR HOME BUILDERS HAVE BEEN BUILDING HOMES SINCE THE END OF WORLD WAR II.

They can offer quality control and building standards that are hard to duplicate on a job site. A host of other custom fabricators can make everything from premanufactured roof trusses to panels that contain drywall on the interior and sheeting and siding on the outside. They are capable of custom-building any truss thickness and insulation you specify. Many will both wire and plumb their panels. They also manufacture floor and roof modules.

STRUCTURAL INSULATED PANELS

Structural insulated panels (SIPs) are manufactured by a number of companies in standard configurations, and most will custom-build to your specifications. A growing and important part of the construction industry, SIPs are used in commercial buildings, barns, domestic housing, modular homes, travel trailers, and cabins. They can be engineered for almost any stress load or application. Built in factory conditions, they exhibit excellent quality control, accurate sizing, and great design flexibility. A great choice of materials is available for both the weather face and the interior surface, as well as the type of insulation used.

Companies that manufacture SIPs usually fall into two categories:

➤➤ **Companies that specialize in structural panel manufacture alone.**
These companies make component panels for job sites or whole-house builders.
They offer a great variety of design and engineering options as well as a menu
of fabrication materials. A number of choices are available for the weather surface,
the interior surface, the strutting material, and insulation. They can custom-
build panels, or a buyer can choose from a variety of premanufactured options.

➤➤ **Companies that are whole-house builders.** These companies offer a
complete panelized or modular system for building. They either manufacture
their own panels or purchase them from specialty manufacturers. Floors,
walls, and ceilings may be manufactured as flat panels and erected at the
building site. Or the cabin may be manufactured in discrete units — bathrooms, kitchen, bedrooms, and so on — that are assembled with the use of a
crane at the building site. Most modular construction methods include electrical wiring, heating and cooling ducts, water pipes, and other utility components already incorporated into the panels.

MODULAR KITCHENS AND BATHS

Even if you're not interested in having your entire cabin constructed with SIPs
or by a modular home builder, you may be interested in having a premanufactured kitchen or bathroom. Some companies specialize in manufacturing such
modules. These units are ready to go, with plumbing and electrical lines already
in place. They are situated with a crane, and the water, sewer, and electrical lines
are connected. Some are conventional stud-and-panel construction, and others
are molded fiberglass. Yet others use a combination of construction methods.
Because a lot of the plumbing and electrical work in a cabin construction project
takes place in bathrooms and the kitchen, you may be able to save yourself both
time and money by using these premanufactured units.

I'm intrigued by the kitchen and bathroom units I see in RVs and travel trailers. Since the end of World War II, RV and travel trailer manufacturers have
been fiercely competing with each other for sales, which has led to significant
improvements in their equipment, appliances, power supplies, and accessories.
Many of the sleek new one-piece kitchen and bathroom units designed for this
industry would adapt easily and well for small cabins.

SPECIAL CONSIDERATIONS

Think through the following considerations carefully if you're interested in using manufactured panels as a construction method:

➤ **Cost.** Making panels in a factory setting is faster and more accurate than stick building (traditional building with stud walls). Labor costs are an important aspect of any building project. Which is cheaper? A good and thorough design process pays off here. Take a set of plans to several modular builders and traditional stick-building contractors and ask for quotes on costs.

➤ **Finding a modular builder.** You may not have much trouble locating a whole-house modular home builder in your area. Finding a company that will manufacture just SIPs or certain modular components may be more difficult. Here in Pennsylvania, several modular home builders make panel or modular components. Most will not stop their assembly lines for a small job; with enough lead time, however, they will schedule a small job in one of their slow periods or between their normal production schedules.

➤ **Crane access.** Very steep or rocky sites do not lend themselves to placing a crane to lift the panels off a truck and put them in place. Marshy sites near lakes may be too soft for the crane to stabilize itself on its outriggers. Access roads need to be adequate for both the crane and flatbed tractor trailers to access the site.

➤ **Design concerns.** Some architectural designs may not lend themselves to modularization. Most panel builders use conventional 2×4 and 2×6 wall studs with either plywood panels or drywall. Contemporary design ideas may be best implemented by conventional stick-building techniques.

➤ **Time.** With modular construction, much of the work is performed in a factory and not on the cabin site. This work can be carried out during the winter, and the panels or components can be stored until needed. Most of the on-site construction can be accomplished in about a week. Some modular home builders can build a cabin and transport it on a trailer frame in the same manner as the mobile and modular homes they manufacture. The result is truly an instant cabin. Everything is in place: baths complete, kitchen cabinets and appliances in place, walls painted, and carpet or flooring already installed. They install the unit on a foundation and connect the utilities, and you're good to go.

SHIPPING CONTAINERS

An intriguing idea is the use of shipping containers as the base module for the cabin construction. Shipping containers are designed to be structurally strong. In normal use, they are filled with cargo and stacked on top of each other. Most containers are designed to handle a gross weight of over 60,000 pounds. This ability greatly exceeds the demands of cabin builders.

Shipping containers are usually about 8 feet wide and 20 or 40 feet in length. They are available in both insulated and uninsulated versions. Most have a head clearance of 7 feet 8½ inches; high cube containers are 8 feet 6 inches high.

Shipping containers are designed to lock onto a trailer for easy transport. Used shipping containers can be purchased, moved to the cabin site, and assembled into a living space. An on-site crane can lift them off the trailer and put them in place. An almost endless variety of spaces can be made by either stacking the containers or placing them side by side. With the addition of a roof, you have a cabin.

Using shipping containers poses an interesting design challenge: how to make a cabin based on them not look like a series of old trailers stacked together. The best approach is to use the containers as the bones of a cabin and use conventional building materials in combination with them. Conventional 2×4 framing fits well with the rectangular shape of shipping containers. Most manufacturers of roofing trusses will custom-design trusses to fit your needs. Roofing materials such as raised rib metal or corrugated metal roofing used as siding could be chosen to match the look of the shipping containers. With the addition of trussed roofing and conventional wall systems, shipping containers can become an integral part of interesting cabin designs. Also try to incorporate large windows to cure the boxy feel of the containers.

Four examples of shipping-container cabins are offered at the end of this chapter. (See also the design on page 206.) They combine used shipping containers with traditional wood framing. In all of the designs, the utilities, including the kitchens and bathrooms, are housed in the shipping container portion of the cabin. The shipping containers could be modified and internal structures built before the containers are moved to the cabin site. Kitchen and bathroom units could be installed, partition walls built, and utilities, insulation, and fixtures installed prior to transportation to the site. Preparation of the shipping containers could take place in the off-season and greatly accelerate the building process on the cabin site. Preparing shipping containers close to home would save a considerable amount of transportation time and driving expense.

A number of companies specialize in selling used shipping containers. A simple search on the Internet can point you in the right direction.

My Junkman's Container Home

From the mid-1970s through the mid-1980s I owned a farm, and there I did my first experimentations with wind power. I befriended a local junk dealer, who was an incredible source of cheap components for building wind pumps and generators. He was also my first introduction to the concept of using shipping containers as building units.

My junkman lived in his junkyard in two 45-foot tractor-trailer containers situated side by side, with a pitched roof over them and a deck on the rear.

This setup created 720 square feet of living space at virtually no cost to him. His water came from the roofs of his storage sheds and was stored in a cistern, and he heated with wood. He lived a simple and comfortable life on a disabled veteran's pension in his container home — it was amazing to behold.

MODERNIST SHIPPING CONTAINER CABIN

This cabin is designed to accommodate solar-electric panels and the large bank of batteries necessary for energy storage. If used in seasons other than summer, some form of heat, such as gas space heating or hot water recirculation, will need to be added.

Features

374 square feet

Full kitchen

Three-quarter bath

Sleeps 2 or 3

Utilizes one 40-foot shipping container

Adaptable to being off the grid

FULL KITCHEN:
a welcome amenity in any small cabin, and especially for those that will house families with children.

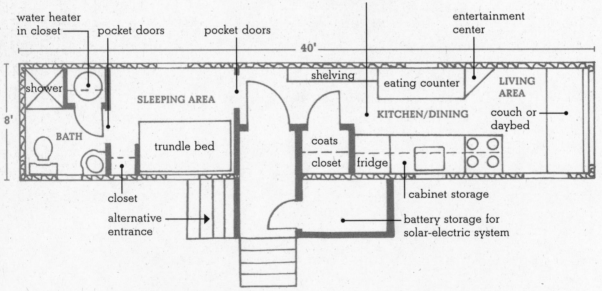

water heater in closet — pocket doors · pocket doors

entertainment center

40'

shelving

shower

SLEEPING AREA

eating counter

LIVING AREA

8'

BATH

KITCHEN/DINING

couch or daybed

trundle bed

coats

closet   fridge

closet

alternative entrance

cabinet storage

battery storage for solar-electric system

⧓⧓⧓ = shipping container

**POSSIBLE RV
AIR CONDITIONER**

SOLAR PANELS:
roof angle and
position flexible.

**POSSIBLE RV
AIR CONDITIONER**

ENTRANCE PORCH:
can be varied in design
and position to take
maximum advantage
of the sun.

CLEAR CREEK SHIPPING CONTAINER CABIN

This simple cabin design can be varied in style and size based on the frame that is added to the shipping container module. Because of the small scale of this cabin, a very small woodstove will comfortably heat it even in cold weather.

Features
480 square feet
Full kitchen
Full bath
Sleeps 2 to 4
Utilizes one 20-foot shipping container

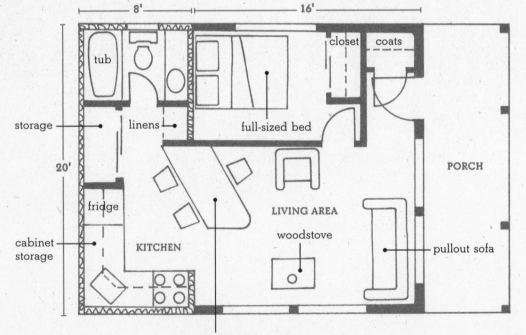

DINING TABLE: could have stools that tuck underneath, so the table doubles as an island counter for the kitchen.

= shipping container

SHIPPING CONTAINER: makes up the back end of the cabin.

ADD-ON FRAME: the size and layout of the add-on frame can be varied to suit the needs of the cabin owner.

WINDOWS: big banks of windows make the interior seem quite open to the outdoors.

TWO-STORY SHIPPING CONTAINER CABIN

This roomy cabin contains two bedrooms and two full baths. Space heating is provided by a wood-burning stove. With a propane-fired refrigerator, cookstove, and water heater, this cabin would work well off the grid.

Features
720 square feet
Full kitchen
Two full baths
Sleeps 4 to 6
Utilizes three 20-foot shipping containers
Adaptable to being off the grid

OVER-SINK KITCHEN WINDOW: a classic feature for kitchens large and small, giving anyone standing at the sink a view out into the open.

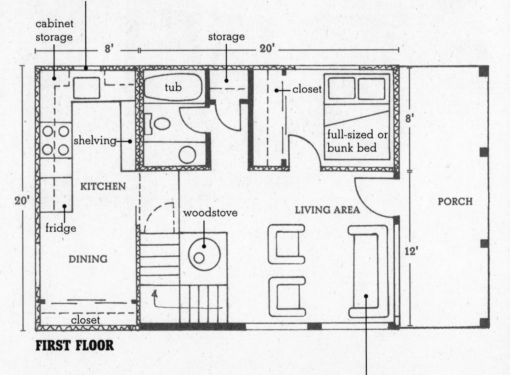

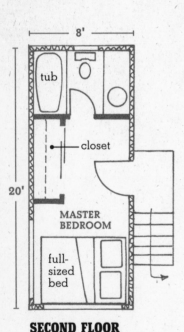

PULLOUT SOFA: provides sleeping space for extra guests.

 = shipping container

SECOND-FLOOR MASTER BEDROOM: takes up one entire shipping container.

PITCHED ROOF: could support solar panels if oriented to the south.

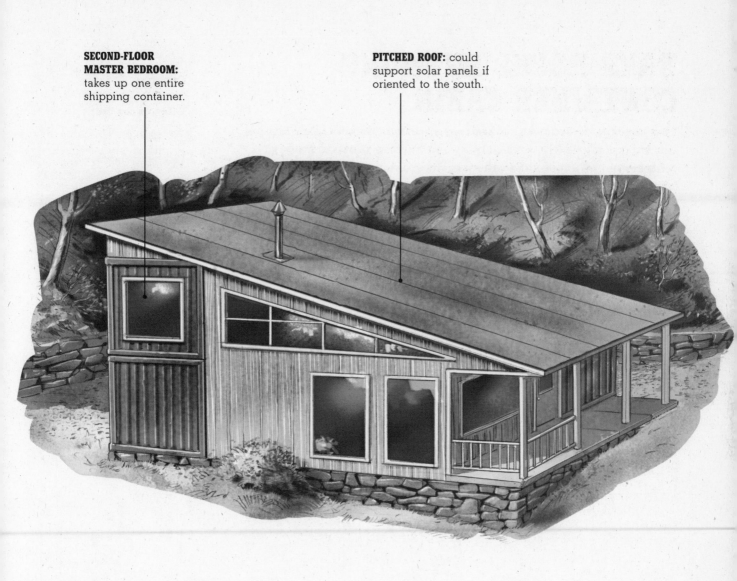

BAER ROCKS SHIPPING CONTAINER CABIN

This larger three-bedroom cabin sleeps up to eight people. Space heating is easily and efficiently provided by a wood-burning stove. Adding a gas refrigerator and a cook stove will make this cabin well suited to remote building sites or off-the-grid applications.

Features
800 square feet
Full kitchen
Full bath
Sleeps 6 to 8
Utilizes two 20-foot shipping containers
Adaptable to being off the grid

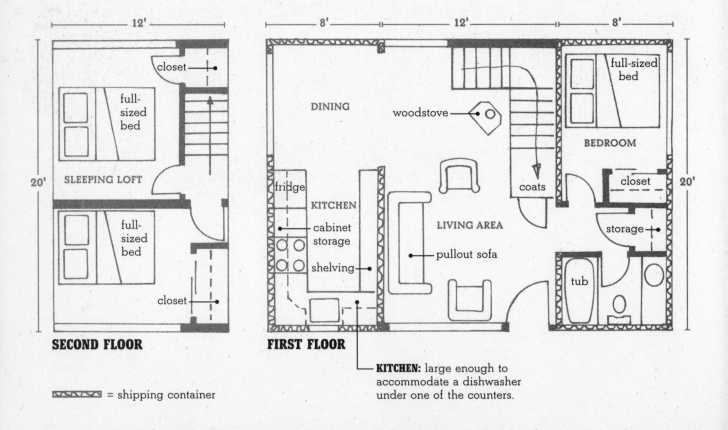

SECOND FLOOR

12'

20'

closet

full-sized bed

SLEEPING LOFT

full-sized bed

closet

FIRST FLOOR

8'   12'   8'

20'

DINING

woodstove

full-sized bed

BEDROOM

coats

closet

fridge

KITCHEN

cabinet storage

shelving

LIVING AREA

pullout sofa

storage

tub

KITCHEN: large enough to accommodate a dishwasher under one of the counters.

〰〰 = shipping container

SLEEPING LOFT: adds sleeping space for four people without greatly increasing the construction cost.

PITCHED ROOF: could support solar panels if oriented to the south.

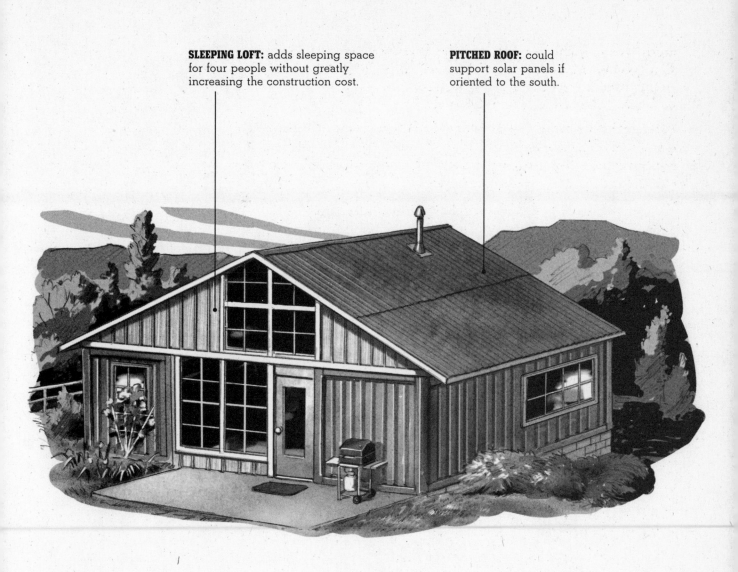

GETTING THE MOST FROM BUILDING MATERIALS

WHEN BUILDING A CABIN, EVERYONE WANTS TO KEEP THE COST TO A MINIMUM. THE TWO MAJOR COST FACTORS ARE MATERIALS AND LABOR.

And the amount of labor a cabin will require is determined, at least to some extent, by your decisions regarding building materials. My strategy for getting the most from building materials follows five rules:

1. Plan/design well. The old adage is "Measure twice, cut once." I add the mantra, "Design, design, design."

2. Shop well. Finding materials is as much a part of design as is drafting plans. I tend to look for odd lots, off-color lots, and surplus materials, because they are available at prices well below retail. It pays to put in the time to look for just the right materials at just the right price. The Internet can be helpful here — you can use it to check prices of any materials or fixtures you're considering to make sure that you're getting a good deal.

3. Stage the project. Don't be in a hurry to purchase everything you need all at once. Instead, purchase the materials you want when you can get them at a good price, then store them until you need them.

4. Buy used materials and fixtures when possible. Used or recycled materials can cost less than new ones. It makes ecological sense to work with them rather than having new materials manufactured. And sometimes "used" can equate to an interesting period-piece fixture or authentically timeworn material.

5. Make your own labor cost-effective. You most likely will be doing some of the work yourself. Plan well, get cost quotes from contractors, and know your own skills so that you can make cost-effective decisions about which parts of the work you should do yourself and which parts should be left to contractors.

LABOR DECISIONS

Most small cabin builders want to perform at least some of the labor them-selves. As part of your planning, evaluate your options for each aspect of the labor. Here again, cost-effectiveness plays an important role. In this case, cost-effectiveness is determined by the balance between time and money. If you have the time, doing the work yourself can save money. If you're short on time, however, or if hiring a professional would result in significant time savings, it may be more cost-effective to hire the job out.

For example, say I need to install footers for the foundation of my cabin. The first task would be to excavate so the footers can be set into the ground. I have several options:

➤ I could dig by hand — cheap but labor intensive and time-consuming.

➤ I could hire or rent a backhoe to dig the footers in an hour or two.

➤ I could buy a backhoe and dig them myself.

Purchasing a backhoe to dig a few footers makes no sense unless I have a future use for the backhoe — and that would have to be a significant future use to make it worth the money. Digging footers by hand might consume most of a summer's available work time. Hiring a backhoe and operator or even rent-ing the equipment makes the most sense. Of course, to use a backhoe I would need the skills to operate it. It's impractical to think I could learn to operate a complex piece of machinery I have never used and do a good, professional job the first time out.

The most cost-effective way to get those footers dug would be for me to hire a backhoe and operator and have him dig the footers for me. As I would with any contractor I hire, I would bargain with the backhoe operator for the best price:

➤ Contact several operators and get price quotes.

➤ Ask around. Most locals know who does the best work at the best price.

➤ Give the contractor a time frame in which to get the work done.

For the backhoe operator, I would probably plan to pour footers after the last frost of the spring season. The last frost in my area is in early May. I would

Building with Piers

The pole building indus-try has developed precast steel-reinforced concrete piers that can be used as foundations for many types of buildings. Like full foundations, they keep pressure-treated lumber from ground contact, but they are much easier to install — any reasonably handy person should be able to do it. The piers are available in various thick-nesses and lengths and usually have steel mount-ing plates on top, which makes it easy to attach the floor decking to them.

How you set the piers will be largely determined by your local building codes. In general, the process is as follows: Dig holes by hand or with a backhoe. Purchase bags (at least one bag per hole) of dry concrete mix from a building supply center. Mix the bagged concrete on-site and pour a bag into each hole. Spread the mix out into a bottom "plate," about 4 inches deep and reinforced with steel rods (rebar). After the concrete hardens, stand a pier in each footer hole on top of the concrete ➤

plate. True it up, plumb it, brace it in place, then backfill the footer holes. Keep the bracing in place at least until you've installed the floor decking for the cabin.

approach a backhoe operator in February with the stipulation that I needed the footers to be dug by May 5th. This would give him some flexibility as to how and when he gets the job done. The greater the flexibility you can give a contractor, the more likely you are to get a good price.

As far as the footers themselves, I also have a number of options:

➤ I could hire a contractor to install them.

➤ I could build forms (the wood that holds the concrete in place) and pour the concrete myself. (In this case, would I hand-mix the cement or hire a ready-mix truck?)

➤ I could install premanufactured piers, each on top of a small concrete pad that I would mix and pour myself.

Obviously a contractor doing the work takes little of my time but is the most expensive way to go. Building the forms myself and pouring them is the least expensive but the most time-consuming. Using salvaged plywood to build the forms would be a further savings; hiring a ready-mix truck would detract from the savings. The third alternative is probably my best choice.

After I install the footers I would plan to backfill by hand; with the soil loosened by the backhoe, it wouldn't be too difficult, and I could backfill on my own schedule.

SHOPPING AND STAGING

When I'm designing and building a cabin, or even just replacing a kitchen or bathroom, I spend a lot of time and energy in the thinking/design stage. I do drawings and make notes. Then I get to the work of obtaining the materials and fixtures I need. I look online and at local building supply houses to see what materials are available. I ask a lot of questions of suppliers, builders, and friends. And then I start shopping.

When I design I like to focus on design, when I'm shopping I like to focus on shopping, and when I build I like to focus on construction. Staging a project — purchasing materials as you find them and storing them until you're ready to begin construction — allows you to focus on each aspect of the project in its turn, and when you get down to the work of building, you don't have to keep running out to the supply house.

I tend to look for odd-lot, surplus, or recycled materials that can be purchased for a discount; with a little time and work I can get excellent materials at a wallet-friendly price. The Internet is a good place to get an idea of what various items are selling for. That way I know whether or not I'm getting a bargain.

I also try to work with local materials whenever possible. They tend to be less expensive than materials that have to be trucked in from elsewhere, and working with local suppliers is good for the local economy. Plus there's a certain cachet to being able to say that your cabin uses, say, locally milled lumber, locally quarried stone, or local artisan hardware. Look around the area where you are building. Look for local materials manufacturers or suppliers. Here in Pennsylvania is an active logging industry with lumber available from many small sawmill operations. Pennsylvania also still produces slate, which is a viable alternative to ceramic tile. Getting slate tile seconds at a quarry and hauling them yourself would be a low-cost way to tile a kitchen, foyer, or bathroom.

RECYCLED BUILDING MATERIALS

Companies everywhere specialize in used building materials and fixtures. Sometimes these used materials are "funkier" than what's available on the current market. Sometimes they're less expensive. But the cheapest option is not always the best option! I like the term *cost-effective*. Cost-effectiveness considers the cost, design utilization, and usefulness of the item. For example, a new bathroom faucet may cost more than a used one. But the used one may have pitted chrome and valve seats and may need to be replaced in a few years. In this case, the cost-effective approach would be to buy a new fixture.

The thing to do is weigh the costs and merits of the used materials against those of the new materials. Be sure to consider several costs:

➤ **Loss rate.** The loss rate is how much material you'll lose in preparing it for new construction. When recycling lumber or siding, for example, a lot of trimming will be necessary; you should expect about a 20 percent loss rate. Also plan to pull a lot of nails and ruin a few saw blades on hidden nails. The loss rate can vary greatly depending on the quality of the material and how it was handled when removed from the original site.

➤ **Purchase price.** Old, funky, and beautiful light fixtures or entrance doors may cost more than the new equivalent. Old barn beams are worth their weight in gold. New timber cut at a local sawmill may make more sense.

Storage for Staging

If you don't have adequate storage space for the materials and fixtures you've purchased, a rental storage unit may make a lot of sense. I live in a suburban neighborhood, and a pile of materials next to my garage for several months would cause concern among my neighbors. I once bought a new display kitchen from a local kitchen and bath design company for a fraction of its value. They were upgrading their display units and needed to clear out the previous year's design ideas. Part of the deal was that I would remove it myself and haul it away on a tight schedule. I rented a self-storage unit and stored it there for several months. This worked out great — for a few dollars a week I was able to store the kitchen until I was ready to install it.

Things Not to Recycle

Don't attempt to recycle old wiring or fuse boxes. The risk of shock or fire is too great.

Look at old woodstoves or potbellied stoves carefully. Make sure they are sound and replacement parts are available. You can be sure that if your stove is going to break down, it will do so when it is being heavily used in the middle of winter, which is a terrible time to find replacement parts or to replace the stove. I have a nearly 60-year-old Franco-Belge coal stove in my house. It still burns well and is the heart of my auxiliary heating system. Before I installed it, though, I made sure I could get parts for it from a local stove dealer.

➤➤ **Energy efficiency.** Old windows may be charming but not very energy efficient. The addition of storm windows and doors may be necessary.

➤➤ **Lead paint.** Assume that surfaces painted before the late 1960s contain lead paint. The paint will need to be removed or completely covered to be safe.

➤➤ **Insect infestation.** Look carefully for insect or termite infestation. The last thing you want is to build termites into your new cabin.

I grew up in the Pocono Mountains of Pennsylvania. There, and throughout much of Appalachia, cabins were commonly built to utilize either house trailers or travel trailers. A trailer would be hauled to a building site and set up as part of the cabin. Although I find old house trailers dumped in the woods to be ugly and an ecological sin, it is possible to purchase used house trailers very inexpensively. The components — kitchen, bath, heating system, electrical panels, windows, doors — could be reclaimed and incorporated into a well-designed cabin. The shell (which is poorly insulated anyway) could then be hauled to a landfill. Older house trailers are notorious for poor construction, poor insulation, and flat roofs that almost always leak. The in-line design necessary for trailers to be transported by highway is not good design and does not use space well. Saving what is reusable and incorporating it into good design is both cost-effective and good for the environment.

Building with used materials can certainly reap both financial and aesthetic rewards, but doing so can be time-consuming. For example, getting used clapboard siding from a demolition site, hauling it home, and spending your free time over the winter pulling nails and trimming may, or may not, be a good strategy for you. For it to work you need three things:

➤➤ **Time spent reclaiming the lumber, even priming it ahead of time.** Labor is expensive if you hire someone to do this. If you work a 40-hour week and commute to work, time is a factor. What you don't want is a beautiful cabin and no friends or family to share it with.

➤➤ **A truck to haul it in, or at least a good friend with a truck.** Transportation in the form of a hired truck is expensive. I've hauled many appliances for friends in exchange for a helping hand when I needed it. Everybody benefits, and working together helps generate a sense of community.

➤➤ **Somewhere to store the lumber and to work on it.**

COMPACT & EFFICIENT UTILITIES & APPLIANCES

THE DECISIONS YOU MAKE ABOUT UTILITIES AND APPLIANCES WILL PLAY A LARGE ROLE IN HOW YOU END UP USING YOUR CABIN. WITH THOUGHTFUL CONSIDERATION AND PLANNING, THE INVESTMENT YOU MAKE IN THIS EQUIPMENT WILL HELP YOUR CABIN TO BE A SPACE-EFFICIENT, RESOURCE-EFFICIENT, ENERGY-EFFICIENT, AND ENJOYABLE SPACE.

Efficient — that's the key consideration here. Efficiency adds to the great pleasure of cabin life through simplifying household work, reducing operating costs, and limiting environmental impact, allowing cabin dwellers to feel right at home in their little home.

Thankfully for today's cabin owners, many, many options exist for the necessary utilities, namely power, heat, water, and sewage. Appliances are a similar story: whether full-sized or downsized, a vast range of styles and applications is available.

USING RV COMPONENTS

Both a revolution and an explosion have occurred in equipment, appliances, and other components for RVs. Most RV components are scaled down in size and designed to operate on multiple fuels. They are also designed to withstand the rigors of trailering, being operated for short periods of time, and being shut off for months. Since most cabin owners subject their appliances to the same rigors, these appliances are an ideal choice, and you'll find a lot of references to them in this chapter.

Unlike most households, which operate on the 110- to 120-volt alternating current (AC) of the conventional electricity grid, most RVs utilize 12-volt direct current (DC) electricity. They make use of lighting, appliances, televisions, fans, and other electrical components that have been designed to operate on 12-volt DC current. These electrical systems include heavy-duty 12-volt batteries that can power their DC components. They also usually have an inverter that, when RVs are plugged in to the grid, can transform standard AC to DC electricity and charge the RV batteries. Many of these inverters are designed to automatically switch an RV from grid power to battery power when the grid fails. Electrical inverter systems adapt well to use in small cabins. An inverter/battery system can be combined with a solar electric panel system and/or a wind turbine to power a small cabin completely off the grid. (See chapter 7 for more details.)

Manufacturers of RVs also produce innovative, multifunctional furniture that adapts well for use in small cabins. For example, dining space is provided in many RVs through a dinette booth. The table portions of these dinettes fold down, converting the dinette into a bed that varies in size from a single to a queen-sized bed. Most dinettes are designed to offer additional storage space under their seating section.

Many RVs have portable gas stoves; they can be moved from indoors to outdoors for hot-weather cooking. Space- and energy-efficient RV refrigerators can operate on multiple fuels. Water systems have become very sophisticated: Bathrooms are one piece, incorporating toilets, lavatory sinks, and showers, and some even offer tubs! Hot water systems are becoming point-of-use systems and therefore very energy efficient.

Other potentially useful RV accessories include roll-up awnings that can be bolted directly to a cabin exterior wall; they retract for secure storage when not in use. Portable appliances, folding tables and furniture, bedding, bath accessories, dinnerware, and kitchenware designed for RV use adapt well to small cabins.

The three plans that follow rely heavily on RV power systems and design innovations. You'll find that many of the plans in chapter 1 call for RV components as well.

From RVs to Cabins

Usually once or twice during the winter, I attend local RV shows. I'm not in the market for a new travel trailer; I like to see the new innovations this very competitive industry is introducing to the world. And each year in February, when I have to haul my travel trailer to my local travel trailer dealer for a yearly inspection, I arrange to arrive at the moment the dealer opens for business and wait until the inspection is finished. I'm always interested in anything new I might see in trailer design, and while the inspection is taking place I usually wander through the sales lot admiring the offerings.

This year, I saw at the back of the sales lot a damaged trailer that had been struck from behind by a car. Other than this damage it was in very good shape. I asked about it and was told that the insurance company had declared the trailer a total loss and the owner was trying to dispose of it. I passed this information on to a friend who was planning to build a cabin in the spring. He purchased the trailer from the insurance company for two thousand dollars and made plans to incorporate the kitchen, bathroom, electrical control system, plumbing and water supply, and furniture into his cabin. After removing what he wanted from the trailer, he donated the damaged shell to a local volunteer fire company to be used for firefighting practice.

side view

top view

A folding table whose cabinet doubles as pantry storage is just one of many space-efficient RV innovations that would work well in a compact cabin.

RV-BASED MICRO CABIN

If your idea of a great vacation is being outdoors as much as possible, this cabin is for you. It's tiny but complete, with a half bath and kitchen. The space heating could be provided by a gas space heater or a furnace designed for a small travel trailer.

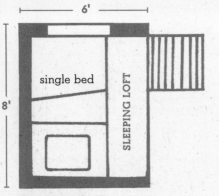

SECOND FLOOR

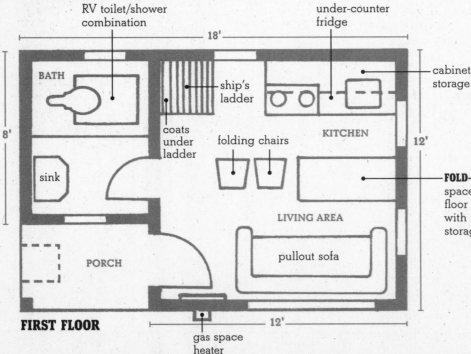

FIRST FLOOR

Features		
192 square feet		
Half kitchen		
Half bath		
Sleeps 1 to 3		
Relies on RV components		
Adaptable to being off the grid		

RV Components		
12-volt DC electrical system		
12-volt DC water pump		
12-volt DC lighting system		
12-volt deep-cycle batteries		
Shower/toilet combination		
Multifuel refrigerator		

FOLD-UP TABLE: provides dining space without detracting from floor space; could be combined with a cabinet for pantry storage.

SLEEPING LOFT: provides extra sleeping space without adding much extra cost or taking away from floor space.

SOLAR-ELECTRIC PANELS: oriented to face south to maximize solar power.

BATTERIES: for the solar-electric system are stored under the porch.

RV-BASED FORKSVILLE CABIN

The ceiling height in this cabin is 10 feet, which makes the interior feel much larger than 200 square feet. The full-sized Murphy bed folds up against the wall during the day, increasing the usable space inside. The solar panels allow this cabin to be used in areas where traditional electrical service is not available. The cabin's length and width allow it to be constructed off-site and trailered to the cabin site.

Features

200 square feet

Half kitchen

Three-quarter bath

Sleeps 2

Relies on RV components

Adaptable to being off the grid

Can be built off-site and trailered in

RV Components

12-volt DC electrical system

12-volt DC water pump

12-volt DC lighting system

12-volt deep-cycle batteries

Shower unit

Multifuel refrigerator

LP gas furnace

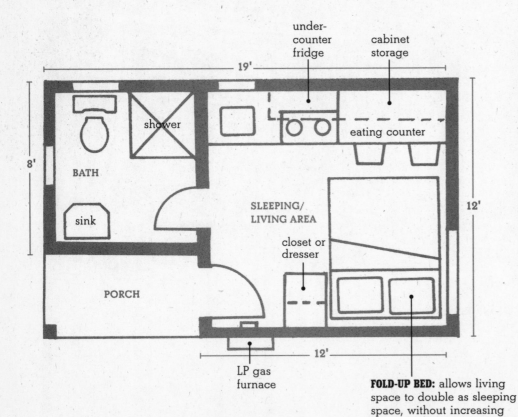

under-counter fridge

cabinet storage

eating counter

shower

BATH

sink

SLEEPING/ LIVING AREA

closet or dresser

PORCH

LP gas furnace

FOLD-UP BED: allows living space to double as sleeping space, without increasing floor space.

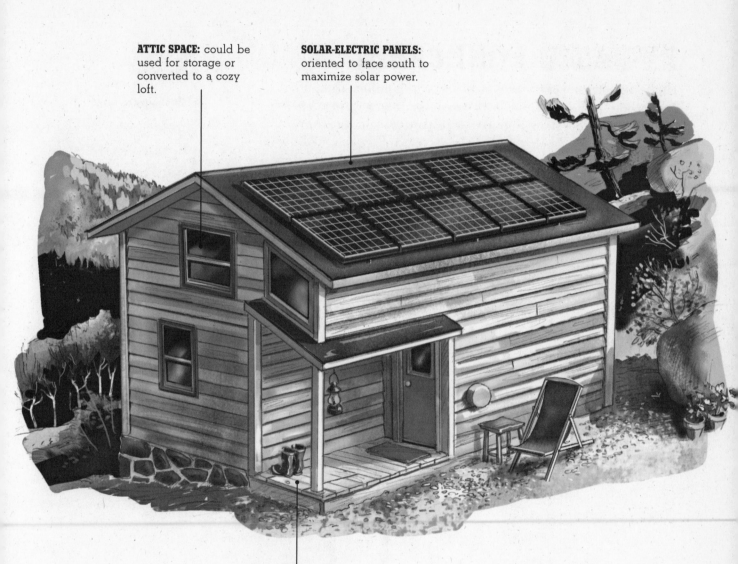

ATTIC SPACE: could be used for storage or converted to a cozy loft.

SOLAR-ELECTRIC PANELS: oriented to face south to maximize solar power.

BATTERIES: for the solar-electric system are stored under the porch.

RV-BASED MINI CABIN

This compact cabin easily sleeps two and, with a pullout sofa, can accommodate up to four. With two closets, two rows of kitchen cabinets, and other storage options, it also offers plenty of room for stowing your belongings.

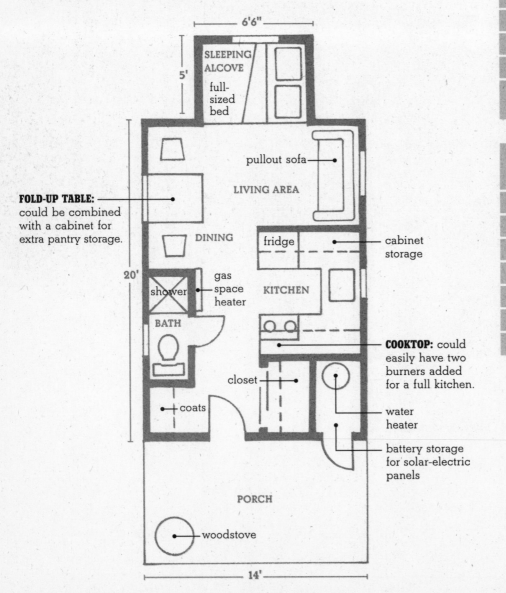

FOLD-UP TABLE: could be combined with a cabinet for extra pantry storage.

6'6"

5'

20'

14'

SLEEPING ALCOVE
full-sized bed

pullout sofa

LIVING AREA

DINING

fridge

cabinet storage

shower

gas space heater

KITCHEN

BATH

closet

COOKTOP: could easily have two burners added for a full kitchen.

coats

water heater

battery storage for solar-electric panels

PORCH

woodstove

Features

313 square feet

Three-quarter kitchen

Half bath

Sleeps 2 to 4

Outdoor woodstove

Relies on RV components

Adaptable to being off the grid

RV Components

12-volt DC electrical system

12-volt DC water pump

12-volt DC lighting system

12-volt deep-cycle batteries

Shower

Multifuel refrigerator

Hot water heater

SOLAR-ELECTRIC PANELS: oriented to face south to maximize solar power.

SLEEPING ALCOVE: provides storage with an overhead shelf and under-bed drawers or boxes.

OUTDOOR WOODSTOVE: great for cooking outdoors in summer or enjoying porch life in cold weather.

HEATING

Most cabins require some form of heating system, and the type of heating system you choose is an important decision in cabin design. A great number of heating stoves with very different design features and aesthetic appearances are available on the market. The major differentiator among them is the heating fuel they use. Wood, coal, or wood/coal stoves are a frequent choice among cabin owners. Other types of heating stoves should also be considered: liquid petroleum (LP) or natural gas, open or closed flame, vented or unvented, space heaters, kerosene heaters, and electric heaters.

Though you could, of course, install a traditional furnace-based system such as you might find in most homes, that machinery can be a bit much for a small cabin, both in terms of its heating capacity and its cost. However, many RVs use LP-fueled, 12-volt DC, hot-air furnaces for heat. These furnaces are small in size and ducted to deliver heat wherever it is needed. Their BTU output is ideal for heating small cabins.

Whatever type of heating unit you choose, it is important to follow the manufacturer's installation instructions. Most local building codes dictate the standard to which these stoves must be installed. Stove sales companies can assist you with obtaining a copy of local codes and standards.

A safe, fireproof area for the stove and a safe chimney system (if the stove needs to be vented) are of utmost importance. Be certain that the stove is a safe distance from any combustible materials, such as walls, window frames, and furniture. The stove manufacturer will specify this distance, which can range from under 1 foot to 3 feet. You might consider investing in a thick masonry surround, which is not just a fire safety precaution but also a way to store heat that will be released into the living space as the fire dies down.

You may also want to consider heat exchange systems that fit into stovepipes. They extract heat from the exhaust gases. Though they do increase the efficiency of the stove system, they may remove too much heat. Some heat is necessary for the convection process that makes chimneys and stovepipes work. Without sufficient convection, combustion gases can back up into living spaces. Systems that draw outside air into the stove for combustion make a lot of sense; warm air is not used for combustion and the fire is isolated from the room air.

Making Do

The first studio I owned was heated with an old wood/coal stove. I built a cement block surround with the block cores open, so air could circulate by convection. As the blocks warmed up, they drew cold air off the floor and warmed it as it passed through their cores. Eventually I tiled the cement blocks with handmade ceramic tile (I was working as a production potter at the time). In addition, I made a heavy square wire basket to fit on top of the stove. I filled this basket with several cubic feet of river rock as a heat sink. The resulting system heated evenly and was cheap to operate. I heated my studio this way for the eight years I lived in that house.

Transoms for Heat Circulation

Designing interior doors to include transoms can assist in the circulation of warm air throughout a cabin. Placing small duct fans in the transoms can help even more; the fans can draw heated air from one space to another. This setup would allow you to use a stove or heater in one room to easily heat adjacent rooms.

A transom window over a doorway can be fitted with a small fan to pull heated air from one room to the next.

Space Heating

In warmer climates, or for cabins used only in warmer seasons, space heating makes sense. Electric or gas space heating is probably the most cost-effective. Catalytic propane heaters, such as those designed for the RV industry, are also good choices. They are small and mount either on or in walls. They come in a variety of sizes determined by their output, which is measured in British thermal units (BTUs). Manufacturers can recommend which size unit you'd want based on the cubic volume of your cabin. I suggest buying a unit with a BTU capacity slightly larger than the formula calls for. This will give you backup capacity for unexpected cold snaps and bring a cold cabin up to temperature when you just arrive.

Hot Water Heat

A novel method to heat small cabins for three-season use is with a hot water heater. A small cabin can usually take care of its hot water needs with a 20-gallon hot water heater. Increasing that capacity to a 40-gallon unit (the size most commonly found in homes) will provide the option of heating a cabin with hot water. Here is how it works: A plumbing tee is placed in the water lines near the hot water outlet pipe and the cold water inlet pipe. This line is then looped through a circulation pump and baseboard hot water heating radiator. The circulation pump is then, in turn, connected to a thermostat. I would also put water valves at beginning and end of this loop, close to where it connects to the hot/cold water lines. The valves allow for the hot water loop to be isolated and shut off from the hot water system. With a drain plug installed at the low point in the hot water heating loop, it can be drained in the winter.

In operation, the thermostat would call for heat and close a relay providing electricity to the circulation pump. The pump would then circulate hot water from the hot water heater through the radiator. When the thermostat was satisfied the circulation pump would shut off. I would not rely on this system in cold weather or for a large cabin; this system is viable for small cabins not used in the cold winter months.

Do You Need Heat?

If you plan to use your cabin only in the summer or live in a warm climate, cabin heating may not be the best way to go. I was recently in southern Brazil. The climate there gets down to around 40 degrees at night in the winter but never as low as freezing. Daytime temperatures climb into the high 60s or low 70s, so virtually none of the houses has any kind of heating system. Electric blankets are popular there. Combined with small electric heaters in bathrooms, the blankets help families in southern Brazil get through the coldest months of July and August.

Hot Water Circulation Heating System

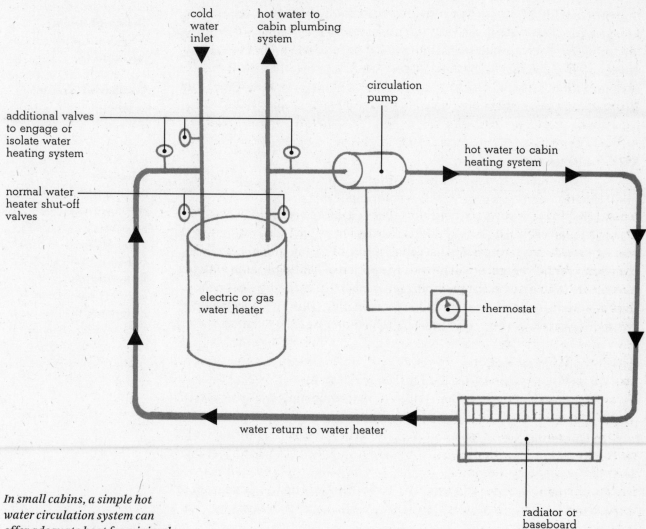

cold
water
inlet

hot water to
cabin plumbing
system

circulation
pump

additional valves
to engage or
isolate water
heating system

normal water
heater shut-off
valves

hot water to cabin
heating system

electric or gas
water heater

thermostat

water return to water heater

radiator or
baseboard
unit

*In small cabins, a simple hot
water circulation system can
offer adequate heat for minimal
cost and infrastructure.*

COOKSTOVES

You can find a vast number of reliable cookstoves on the market. They range from micro-sized backpack cookstoves to large wood/coal kitchen cookstoves. I suggest starting your selection process based on the fuel you intend to burn in this stove. What is available and cheap: wood, coal, gas/propane, or electricity? Then ascertain your need, which is usually the number of burners necessary to cook for a cabin full of people. This number could range from a two-burner RV stove to a six-burner gas or electric range. Do you want an oven? Do you want a microwave? Will you cook mainly inside, or do you plan to grill a lot outside?

RV Cooking Components

Stoves, ovens, and microwaves for RVs are available in sizes that work well in small cabins. And RV gas grills are perfect for small cabin use.

I personally like the three-burner LP gas stoves designed for use in RVs. They can be moved outdoors and reconnected for use in hot weather; the less heat put into a cabin, the less it will need to be cooled. For a number of years, I served as a camp cook for volunteer groups repairing and maintaining hiking trials in state parks and forests. I have cooked for a week for as many as 40 people on three burners. And I also have a small Japanese single-burner LP gas stove I have used for 25 years when I stay in my cabin alone.

Induction Cooktops

A recent interesting advance in cooking technology was first introduced into the restaurant industry: induction cooktops. Induction cooktops utilize the principal of eddy currents to produce heat. The cooking burners are in fact large magnets that operate on home electrical current. When combined with special cookware whose bottoms have an embedded core of iron, they produce heat. The magnetic energy from the cooktop induces a magnetic current in the iron core of the cooking pan. The excited molecules of the pan core then vibrate and produce heat, much in the same way that microwave ovens heat food. Some models of induction hot plates take up very little space and can be moved from place to place as long as an electrical outlet is available. Induction hot plates can be stored in a cabinet, set up on a counter when it's time to cook, and then returned to storage.

One advantage of induction cooking is that the stove does not get hot; the heat is limited to the bottom of cooking pans. The downside is that special cookware and an electrical supply are necessary.

Cookstove Considerations

Choice of fuels:
What is available and cost effective?

Number of people to be fed:
More people = more burners.

Lifestyle:
Is cabin cooking a minimal experience or a chance to be a gourmet?

Convenience:
Do you want to build a fire every time you want to cook?

Summer Kitchens

When farms were being developed in the eighteenth and nineteenth centuries in the Pennsylvania Dutch areas of Pennsylvania, they utilized what were known as summer kitchens. These small buildings were close to the main house and reserved solely for the purpose of cooking in the summertime. This arrangement isolated the cooking heat from the main structure. Some summer kitchens included clothes washing, baking, and even slaughtering facilities. Many Plain People (such as the Amish and Mennonites) still use and build summer kitchens as part of their farmsteads. Cabins that incorporate this idea may make sense in warmer climates.

Electric Cookers

Cabin cooks should consider using pressure cookers and slow cookers. Modern pressure cookers are not the pressure cookers your grandmother used 50 years ago. They are smaller, easier to use, and much safer than the older designs. Pressure cookers greatly reduce cooking times and therefore the use of energy.

Slow cookers, on the other hand, are ideal for cabin living. Most can be plugged into household outlets and placed on a kitchen counter. Load them up in the morning and they need little or no attention during the day. And there's nothing better for breakfast on a cold morning than Irish oatmeal. A slow cooker loaded with Irish oatmeal at bedtime will produce a great breakfast with little work in the morning.

Heating and Cookstove Combinations

Look for heating/cooking stove combinations. This kind of a stove is great in the winter but may put out too much heat in the hot summer months. The way these stoves are designed precludes them from being equally good at space heating and at cooking. Heating stoves are designed to radiate the heat they produce into the room, usually from the front and both sides. Cookstoves are designed to direct the heat upward to the cooking surface. Very few stoves on the market do both chores well.

My stepfather's cabin was heated by an old wood/coal cookstove. It had a warming closet over the cooking surface, a hot water jacket in the firebox, and an oven. It provided heat, hot water, and cooking. This system was comforting, old, and reliable, but it took up a lot a valuable space in the cabin and was impossible to use anytime except in the winter. Nevertheless, that stove was a great pleasure upon return from ice fishing expeditions. You could stand close to the open oven door and get toasty warm in just a few minutes.

FIREPLACES

Fireplaces are very popular in cabins, perhaps because they are an integral part of the image that comes to mind when designers envision a cabin. Fireplaces can provide both heating and cooking facilities. They can be grouped into two major types:

➡ Those built entirely of masonry materials

➡ Those that incorporate metal inserts

Masonry Fireplaces

Fireplaces are usually built of some sort of masonry, such as brick, stone, or concrete block. The masonry mass acts as a heat sink, absorbing heat and then radiating it when the fire dies down. Regardless of the material you choose, the firebox and chimney flue must be built of firebrick, and the flue must have a ceramic liner. The design of a fireplace is critical to its correct operation. For example, the fireplace opening and flue must be sized properly for a fireplace to operate without combustion gases backing up into the room. Smoke shelves and flue dampers are also essential.

Although expensive and time-consuming to construct, masonry fireplaces are a lifetime investment. With regular cleaning, they will last for generations.

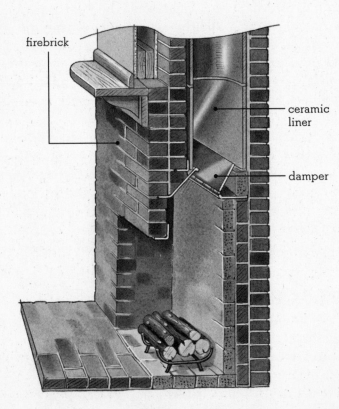

firebrick

ceramic liner

damper

A masonry fireplace evokes classic cabin style. Though in pioneer days fireplaces were always owner-built, and still can be, in most locales their construction is governed by building codes, with strict regulations regarding construction materials and techniques.

Russian Stoves

Russian stoves are essentially fireplaces surrounded by a large mass of masonry and set in a room. They are designed to act as heat sinks and to increase the path of the exhaust gases in order to extract as much heat from them as possible.

Russian stoves are efficient heaters, but they are very expensive to build and take up a lot of living space.

The massive masonry of a Russian stove acts as a heat sink, absorbing heat from the fire within and only slowly releasing it.

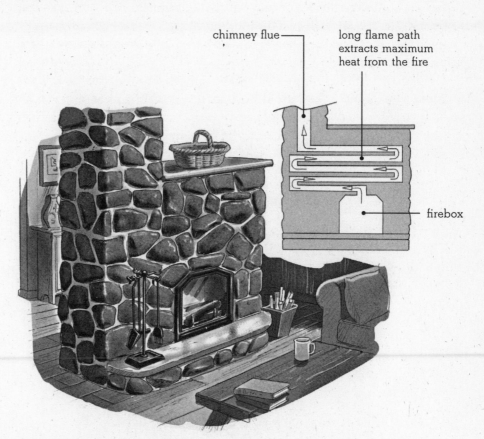

chimney flue

long flame path extracts maximum heat from the fire

firebox

Fireplace Inserts

One drawback of traditional fireplaces is that when any combustion is present in the firebox, the flue must remain open. I have often fallen asleep in a warm cabin only to wake during the night to freezing temperatures because warm air was continually drawn up the flue as the fire went out. If you don't want to have to feed a fire during the night, a fireplace insert may be a better solution.

Fireplace inserts are essentially steel boxes built into fireplaces. They connect to conventional flues or chimneys or exhaust through stainless-steel double-walled pipe. They are usually double-walled, with air circulating between the two walls. Most are equipped with doors and draw their combustion air from outside.

Inserts boast a number of advantages over conventional fireplaces. Since the fire is contained in a steel box, the insert can be surrounded by nonmasonry materials. This allows for a variety of design possibilities for the mantel and reduces overall construction costs. Many fireplace inserts are zero clearance, meaning they can safely be installed in conventional building materials. When coupled with stainless-steel double-walled stovepipe, massive masonry structures are not needed.

Fireplace inserts are fairly good heating devices. Because the fire is isolated from the room by doors and the airflow can be controlled, heat output can be regulated. Many inserts come equipped with circulation fans. Either by convection or fan, inserts draw cool air from the floor and circulate warm air into the living space.

A fireplace insert has all the appeal of a traditional fireplace, with the added benefit of greater choice in materials, potentially reduced cost, and the ability to regulate heat output.

Fire Safety

Make it a policy to inspect your heating stove, cookstove, and fireplace each year. This means a complete inspection of the stove, its firebox, and its operation. Replace any worn parts. Also inspect any stovepipes and chimney caps. Replace any rusted or worn pipe or capping. Clean stoves, chimneys, and stovepipes each year, as creosote buildup can cause chimney fires. I once spent a weekend at a friend's hunting camp. The cabin's only heat source was a large fireplace. Since it was early winter, the fireplace was in constant operation. At about 4 A.M. on a Sunday, a chimney fire broke out. Without a ladder available so we could get to the roof and put the fire out, the fire raged for about an hour before it burned itself out. Though we were lucky in that the fire did not burn the camp down, the heat destroyed the mortar between the bricks. The fireplace had to be entirely dismantled and rebuilt.

Fireplace Cooking

Cooking with a fireplace can be fun, but it is challenging if you are not experienced with handling a fire while you cook. To begin, you need cast-iron cookware; conventional stainless-steel or aluminum cookware will *not* survive fireplace cooking. You'll also need a way to suspend the cookware over the fire. A cast-iron Dutch oven with legs is ideal; it can be placed right over a bed of coals. Some Dutch ovens have flat, recessed lids to hold hot coals. With a little practice, you can bake biscuits, bread, or cakes in these flat-topped Dutch ovens.

Though it has appeal, most of us who live in modern housing may find fireplace cooking too challenging. Crawling out of a down sleeping bag on a frosty morning to start a fire to make coffee can lose its romance after a few mornings. And cooking in a fireplace in the summer is extremely impractical!

AIR CONDITIONERS

Air conditioners are generally considered to be energy hogs, but in really hot or swampy weather, you may want one. A variety of air conditioners are designed to be used in RVs. Most are roof mounted; some are ducted. Sizes are ideal for use in small cabins. If your cabin is off the grid, air conditioners can be operated from a medium-sized portable generator.

REFRIGERATORS

You may want a traditional electric full-sized refrigerator in your cabin. If so, be sure to invest in an Energy Star–rated one.

Check out alternative options for refrigeration. Some refrigerators operate on LP gas, which is great for off-the-grid applications and in locations where grid electricity is unreliable. You might also look at refrigerators from the RV industry, which range in size from 3 to 14 cubic feet. Many operate on multiple fuels, whether 12-volt DC electricity, 120-volt AC electricity, or LP gas.

WATER PUMPS AND TANKS

If you're lucky enough to be building in an area where you can plug in to a town water line, you probably won't need to worry about water pumping. If your cabin water system will rely on a well or other alternative water source, however, you'll likely need a water pump. In either case, you might consider a water storage tank as well, in case of emergency.

Water pumps and tanks designed for RVs can be adapted easily for use in small cabins. They are designed to be easy to winterize and easy to maintain. Most RVs utilize on-demand water pumps that operate on 12-volt DC electricity. These systems can be used with a well or with conventional water sources. Plastic water tanks from 15 to 75 gallons are available for water storage.

WATER HEATERS

Hot-water tanks are available in sizes ranging from 6 gallons to 100 gallons and more. For small cabin usage, tanks of more than 40 gallons are not usually necessary.

Hot-water tanks designed for RVs can be useful in small cabins. They are usually controlled by 12-volt DC electricity and heat with propane. There is no need to operate them constantly; most are designed to reach "hot" in 20 to 30 minutes from startup to shower time. Operating them for a limited number of hours each day saves a great deal of energy.

You might also consider a tankless on-demand hot water heater. These units don't store hot water; they are instead designed to heat water as it's needed (hence, "on demand"). They are usually mounted on the wall of a kitchen or bathroom near where the hot water is needed. Both electric and LP gas versions are available.

WASTEWATER SYSTEMS

Most cabins are built in areas where sewer lines aren't available. In such situations, you may want to consider composting toilets and gray-water recycling systems. Such systems reduce the size and cost of your cabin's septic system.

Composting Toilets

Self-contained composting, or waterless, toilets are a good idea anywhere nutrients from a septic system might leach into the water table, wetlands, or a lake or other waterway. A number of different design systems are available on the market, and most can be incorporated into a conventional bathroom design. All composting toilet systems work on the same principles and have the same objectives:

➻ To handle human waste in accordance with good
sanitation practices

➻ To produce an inoffensive and semidry end product that
can be handled easily

➻ To minimize odor

➻ To contain, immobilize, or destroy organisms that can
cause human disease

The primary component of a composting toilet is the composting reactor or composter, which is connected to one or more waterless or microflush toilets. Most composters use microorganisms to break down wastes. These organisms are aerobic, requiring oxygen to do their job, so the system must have a means to aerate the composter. The composter must also have an exhaust system to remove odors, carbon dioxide, water vapor, and by-products of aerobic composting, and the exhaust should be screened to prevent flies from entering. The system must include a way to drain and manage excess liquid from the composter and an access door so users can remove the composted material when it's ready.

If you want to have a composting toilet in your cabin, consider several factors:

➻ **Self-contained versus centralized.** The choice of which type to select is based on site design, the load on the system (the number of persons using it), and the number of toilets in a cabin. Generally, small cabins use self-contained composting toilets.

➻ **Manufactured or site built.** Manufactured units come ready-made. Just install them and connect any electricity needed. Site-built units can be custom-built and designed to suit the needs of a specific application. (But note that it is generally difficult to get site-built composting toilets approved by zoning code officials.)

➻ **Batch or continuous composting.** Most systems use one or the other system. Continuous composting systems allow urine to continually moisten the process. They also allow the center of the composting pile to heat up through uninterrupted microbial activity. Proponents of the batch composting system say that not continually adding fresh material allows for the composting to take place more thoroughly and uninterrupted. Batch processing allows for unlimited capacity, but such systems require monitoring and their containers need to be exchanged when full.

➤➤ **Active or passive composting systems.** Active systems feature automatic mixers, fans, heaters, thermostats, and so on. These systems may require too much electricity for small off-the-grid systems. Passive systems rely on natural processes over time to do the job. Passive systems are simpler than active systems and therefore require less servicing or maintenance. Active systems, however, can handle a greater quantity of waste.

Outhouses

The old-fashioned outhouse is in fact a waterless composting toilet. It is possible for cabin owners to build an eco-friendly outhouse. A concrete junction box, available from septic system and plumbing supply houses, could be used as an in-ground reservoir for an outhouse. In cabins that are not used excessively or for long periods of time, an outhouse with a leak-proof, in-ground reservoir could be a cost-effective toilet system. (As mentioned earlier, zoning laws may prohibit this type of septic arrangement.)

The outhouse should be downhill from the cabin's water source. In addition, there must be sufficient distance between the water source and the outhouse. Your local building code may specify just how far apart the water source and outhouse need to be, but in general, it's best to place them as far apart as is practical.

If you have ever used an outhouse in the middle of a midwinter night, you know their major flaw. In summer, many outhouses become home to all sorts of creepy-crawly things. However, good building practices can make an outhouse tight enough to eliminate insects, snakes, chipmunks, and other critters. A vent stack from the composting chamber, extending above the roofline, can exhaust odors well away from any human nose. A 3- or 4-inch-diameter vent pipe (PVC pipe or rain gutter pipe works well) extending 3 feet or so above the roofline of the outhouse and painted black can act as a solar vent system. Equip this vent pipe with a cap that will eliminate both rainwater and insects. It will exhaust waste gases and also aid in drawing needed fresh air into the composting chamber.

Catching and Storing Water

In my garage I have installed six 50-gallon, interconnected, blue plastic drums. The drums are arranged against one wall of the garage and support a storage shelving system. I equipped the gutter of my garage roof with a diverter that channels rain water into the drums until they are filled. I use a small submersible fish pond pump and garden hoses to pump that water to where it is needed. I use that water to water my garden, wash my car and truck, and wash my boat after an outing, before I store it. I also use it to fill another barrel I keep near my garden in which I make compost tea as fertilizer. In the winter, I drain the drums to keep them from freezing.

Outhouses can be combined with other outbuilding functions, such as storage of tools or wood. Combining functions saves on building time and materials.

Gray-Water Recycling

Gray water is wastewater from sinks, tubs, and showers, which, unlike wastewater from the toilet or kitchen sink, doesn't contain serious contaminants. It may also include rainwater runoff from your cabin's roof. Gray-water recycling systems are designed to capture this wastewater, filter it, and store it for future use. Though filtered, it should not be consumed. However, it can be used to water a garden or flush a toilet.

Local building codes usually include specifications for the design and installation of gray-water recycling systems. In general, such systems are made up of three components:

➤ A filter to remove any solid matter from the water (the small foam filters used as prefilters for fish ponds adapt well to filtering gray water)

➤ A large holding tank to store the water

➤ A pump and plumbing system to move the gray water to where it is needed

To reduce your system's gray-water load, you can move both showers and sinks outdoors so that they shed their water straight onto the ground. In warm weather this makes a lot of sense.

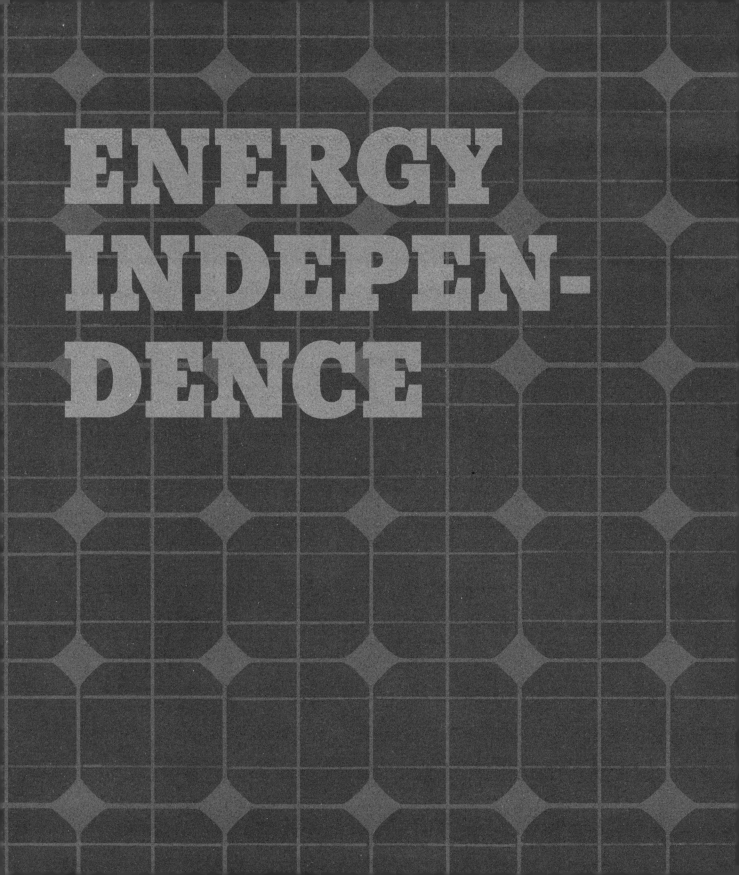

ENERGY INDEPENDENCE

MANY SMALL CABIN BUILDERS ARE ATTRACTED TO OFF-THE-GRID ENERGY SYSTEMS.

They may be building a cabin in an area where conventional electric service is not available or unreliable, or perhaps the idea of living without a utility bill sounds good to them. The sense of energy independence afforded by off-the-grid systems appeals to our pioneer spirit and need to feel in control of our lives.

Small cabins are ideal for adaptation to off-the-grid energy systems. Compared to homes or even larger cabins, they are easier to heat and cool, requiring less energy for either endeavor. They require less lighting and have fewer and generally smaller appliances, therefore consuming less electricity. Bathing facilities are smaller and require less hot and cold water and smaller septic systems. You'll find several designs for off-the-grid cabins at the end of this chapter, and almost all of the designs in chapter 1 can be adapted to be off the grid.

Designing for energy efficiency is an essential aspect of achieving energy independence, and it just makes plain good sense even if you don't intend to live off the grid. We'll talk about ways to improve the efficiency of any cabin later in this chapter.

DESIGNING AN OFF-THE-GRID SYSTEM

Off-the-grid energy systems fall into several general categories:

- ➤ Solar-powered systems

- ➤ Wind-powered systems

- ➤ Water-powered systems

- ➤ Generator-based systems

- ➤ Hybrid systems (utilizing more than one type of alternative energy technology)

The term *off the grid* usually refers to energy systems that provide electricity. Many of these systems can do more than that, however. Solar collectors, for example, can be used to heat water, which in turn can be used to heat a cabin. Wind power can be used to pump water. And these systems may combine various off-the-grid technologies with on-the-grid electrical supplies. They also may be used in conjunction with other alternative technologies, such as heating with wood or using propane (or LP) to power a refrigerator or furnace.

Evaluating Local Conditions

When choosing and designing an off-the-grid system, it is important to design to live not only *in* an environment but also *with* an environment. Local conditions will determine your best course of action. Your building site must have sufficient sun exposure for solar cells to be effective, enough wind for wind generators, and adequate water flow for water-powered generators.

The U.S. Department of Energy provides online wind and solar maps for the entire country. Though a good starting place, the information is only general and conditions at your site might vary greatly. For example, large shade trees on a building site or a site located in a deep valley will influence how much sun is available for solar panels. Furthermore, seasonal changes alter the intensity of both the sun and winds. Winter usually means less sun but more wind. In summer, the reverse is the rule. So if you intend to use your cabin mainly in the winter, wind power may be a good choice. Solar power, on the other hand, may be a better choice if you're going to use your cabin mainly in the summer.

If your site doesn't have good access to sun, wind, or water power, that doesn't mean you can't have at least some independence from the grid. You may in this case need to rely on generators powered by LP or the electric grid.

Most states have county agricultural agents who assist farmers and others with questions and problems pertaining to land use and crops. County agents are not experts in energy use or alternative energy; however, they can be a good resource in directing you to local people or agencies that can help you determine what system will work best in a given locale. State conservation and natural resources departments can also be valuable resources in finding appropriate technologies, as can local college and university architecture and civil engineering departments. The secret is to ask and then ask where else you might look.

A number of companies are in the business of designing and selling off-the-grid systems. Most will offer advice and consultations, as well as custom-

Working with Professionals

Off-the-grid energy systems companies are experts in the design and installation of custom systems. Some specialize in just one type of energy, such as solar or wind power; others have a broader reach. They can advise you about the components you will need and what will work best on your specific site. Unless you're a solar/wind expert yourself, it pays to get the advice of someone who is. Many solar/wind companies can sell you a complete system for less than you would pay for the individual components.

Buy the Best Batteries

My experience has been that batteries are the weak link in off-the-grid electrical systems, having to be replaced every two to three years. So it pays to buy the best batteries you can afford at the time. Most of the companies that sell wind generation and solar electric equipment have batteries available. Some offer batteries specifically manufactured for these applications.

design systems to meet your needs. Local companies are perhaps your best resource, as they will be familiar with local conditions and building codes.

The Basic Setup

Most off-the-grid electrical systems are made up of the following components:

➤➤ **A generation source.** Either solar-electric panels or wind generators, or a combination of the two. It could be water powered. The idea is to generate electricity.

➤➤ **An energy storage system.** Usually a series of deep cycle or golf cart batteries connected to the system. The batteries allow you to store the power you generate for those times when your natural power source (such as sunlight) is not available.

➤➤ **An inverter.** A device that converts the 12-, 24-, or 36-volt DC coming from the storage batteries into usable 110- to 120-volt AC needed by most standard home appliances.

➤➤ **A backup generator.** A generator that can take over when natural conditions fail to produce sufficient electricity to run a cabin and can charge storage batteries. Charging storage batteries with a generator is usually done in the off hours when the noise of a generator running is not bothersome.

➤➤ **An interface connector.** A device that can interface with the conventional power grid. This interface can switch you on or off the grid. A number of hybrid systems use an interface connector to combine grid electricity with on-site generated sources. Some systems can return surplus electrical capacity back to the grid to reduce grid electrical costs.

Sizing the System

Off-the-grid power systems are usually designed by wattage output. Off-the-grid power systems generally range from 300 to 15,000 watts for home or cabin use. Generally you pay for watts. That is, as the capacity to generate and store larger amounts of electricity increases, so does the price. Small systems are inexpensive, but 300 watts is not a lot of electricity. The average household wall outlet has about 1,500 watts of electricity available.

You must carefully calculate the size of the system you need before purchasing and installing off-the-grid components. Energy use is calculated in watts. Appliances have labels listing their watt requirements. To figure out how many watts you need, total the watt requirements of your lighting system; add the requirements of any appliances such as radios, televisions, and refrigerator; and add the requirements of your utility systems, such as your water system and heating system. You probably will not use all of these energy-consuming devices at one time. Your average maximum need may be somewhere between 75 and 80 percent of this number. A system designed to produce enough energy for this number should allow you to live comfortably in an off-the-grid cabin.

Of course, you may need to change your energy use habits. I once had a cabin with a wind generator and storage battery system for its electrical supply. One of my great pleasures was watching the morning news and weather over freshly brewed coffee. The system would not support both the television and the electric coffee maker at the same time, so I wouldn't turn on the television until the coffee was brewed. One day it dawned on me that I could have my coffee and weather too. I bought a plunge-type coffee maker and heated the water for it on my gas stove. It was a simple and small adjustment without any sacrifice of lifestyle.

Flexibility and Growth

A well-designed off-the-grid system should allow some flexibility in how you implement the system. Flexibility is the one single element that makes off-the-grid systems successful over time. A well-designed off-the-grid system should also allow for the possibility of future growth. For example, you should be able to add more storage batteries, more solar-electric panels, or a bigger backup generator. This foresight may mean that some parts of the system have greater capacity than you immediately need. Your system controller and inverter, for example, may be too large for your current needs, but they will allow for the addition of larger or more elements later on.

Installing extra 12-volt wiring circuits and a large control panel before the walls are enclosed will make it easy to add on later; retrofitting wiring into an existing cabin can be time-consuming, expensive, and messy. The mantra of a good off-the-grid system designer is look ahead, plan ahead.

Wind generators are hard to upgrade or replace. If you're investing in wind power, I recommend buying the largest capacity wind generator you can afford and then building up the rest of your system to match over several years.

Heat from Hot-Water Circulation

Alternative energy technologies can function in multiple ways. How you implement them depends on your needs and assets. For example, solar hot water systems provide hot water for bathing and dishes. Solar hot water systems with very large storage tanks can also be used for space heating on cool nights if they are coupled to conventional hot water baseboard units (or even old-fashioned radiators). The system can be gravity-fed or the hot water can be circulated with a small electric pump. If the hot water storage tank is below the level of the baseboard unit or radiator, hot water will rise into the radiator and the cold water will settle and return to the tank in a loop system. A climate with hot, sunny days and cool nights would be an excellent setting for this sort of solar-heated water and nighttime heating arrangement.

Hybrid Systems

Hybrid off-the-grid systems have advantages over systems that rely on a single energy source. A wind generator is only good when the wind blows. A hybrid system of a wind generator and a gas-powered portable generator has an obvious advantage.

Two important factors favor hybrid systems. The first is flexibility: not having to rely on any single element of the system for every need makes the system more flexible and less prone to failure. Second, hybrid systems can take advantage of resources in a way that single-energy systems cannot. A hybrid system can be custom-designed to take advantage of site resources and the specific needs of the cabin designer.

WORKING WITH DIRECT CURRENT

Storage batteries accept and release electricity in the form of DC. Most household appliances run on AC. For this reason most off-the-grid energy systems use an inverter to transform the batteries' DC into household AC.

However, the conversion of DC to AC results in a loss of electrical energy, usually in the form of heat that is ventilated from the inverter. Given the energy loss in conversion and the cost of large-capacity inverters, DC-powered components make a lot of sense. The RV industry has developed a host of lighting fixtures and appliances that operate on 12-volt DC. (For more information about DC components from the RV industry, see chapter 6.)

The major shortcoming of DC systems is that transmitting DC over long distances results in a large energy loss and is therefore impractical. Because the transmission distance of electricity in a home power grid is short, this loss is not usually a factor.

A novel approach to powering a cabin would be to use grid electricity to charge storage batteries. These batteries then would operate a 12-volt DC lighting and appliance system. This may sound like it doesn't make sense, but let's examine it a little further. There are two advantages to this type of system:

➤ The charging can be done in off-peak hours, when grid electricity can be purchased most cheaply.

➤ In remote areas where the grid electrical system is unreliable, this setup provides a consistent, reliable energy source.

Hybrid systems that combine conventional grid-supplied 110- to 120-volt AC energy and locally produced 12-volt DC energy to power DC components offer the least expensive reliable system in remote areas. A friend of mine owns a houseboat and uses this kind of a hybrid system to run his electrical and appliance system, which operates on 12-volt DC. He has installed a large-capacity 12-volt DC alternator on the diesel engine of the houseboat so that the engine can charge his storage batteries while it is operating. The controller/inverter panel of his boat can also be plugged into the grid system when the boat is docked, converting the grid's AC power to DC to power the batteries. Whether he is tied up to his dock or cruising the Chesapeake Bay, his electrical and appliance system operates in the same consistent way.

In a cabin, a similar setup would combine an off-the-grid power system and conventional grid-based electricity. For example, the cabin could be powered by a wind turbine, which charges storage batteries to power DC appliances and utilities. For those times when wind power is low, the cabin would also be tied in to the conventional electrical grid, which would also — through an inverter — charge the storage batteries. (And for those times when wind power is plentiful, the cabin owner might be able to sell power from the cabin's batteries to the electric grid.) The cabin benefits from having redundant power sources, giving the owner both more security and more flexibility.

PASSIVE SOLAR HEATING

Cabin builders who plan to use off-the-grid cabins in colder weather should consider passive solar heating. Passive solar heating systems are passive because they require no energy input. They are distinguished from active solar systems in that active systems require some energy input to power pumps or fans to circulate hot water or move hot air. Passive systems rely instead on two structural features: a large solar glazing area coupled with a heat sink.

For most homes and cabins, a large solar glazing area equates to large glass windows facing a southern exposure. These windows maximize sunlight entering the home, helping to heat it. To minimize heat loss in cold weather, the windows should have a high R factor and be fitted with insulated blinds, shutters, or curtains that can be closed at night. Passive solar cabins usually have roofs with large overhangs that are designed to exclude intense summer sun but allow winter sunlight to enter the cabin.

Traveling Light

I have a small travel trailer that I use in volunteer conservation work. I combine a small gasoline-powered generator with two portable solar-electric panels. The combination of solar-electric panels and the generator has allowed me to live for as much as nine weeks off the grid. On a sunny day, the solar-electric panels do a nice job of charging the trailer batteries. On rainy or cloudy days, I will need to run the generator for about two hours each day to charge the batteries.

The water system in the trailer runs on a 12-volt pump. The lighting and fans are also 12-volt. The stove is LP gas, and the refrigerator is a multiple fuel unit, which usually runs on LP gas. The trailer batteries are two 12-volt deep cycle marine batteries (seconds from a local battery manufacturing company). One I can detach and use in combination with an electric trolling ▸▸

motor for a small boat.
The hot water system is
also LP gas powered. The
electronic ignition system
on this heater is 12 volt.
The furnace in the trailer
is LP gas, controlled with
a 12-volt thermostat and
ignition system. All of
the systems in this trailer
could be duplicated and
produce a reliable utility
system for a small off-the-
grid cabin.

A heat sink is a structure that absorbs heat and releases it slowly. Usually it is a thick energy-absorbing floor in a dark color. Here in Pennsylvania, thick slate floor tiles are an excellent choice; they can be set in a mortar base and act as a natural heat sink. Flagstone tile flooring is another excellent choice. Some passive heating designers use containers filled with water to absorb heat. These containers are usually 50-gallon drums painted black and arranged in a line close to the glazing area. (Such water-filled drums would need to be drained in the winter to avoid bursting during a freeze.) A secondary or gray-water system could be positioned and used as part of a passive solar heating system.

Passive solar systems can be run in reverse and used to provide some daytime cooling. In hot weather, shutters or blinds can be closed to limit solar gain by blocking light from entering during peak daylight hours. The heat sink will absorb much of the heat in the cabin. At night, the building is opened up and the heat sink is allowed to cool.

ENERGY-SAVING IDEAS FOR CABINS

Of course the first step in designing an off-the-grid system — or indeed even an on-the-grid system — should be to minimize your cabin's energy usage. A plan will minimize not only the natural resources you consume, but also your long-term costs.

Many federal, state, and local programs provide tax relief or grants for energy-saving measures homeowners or home builders may take. Ask around to find out what programs are available in your area. The Database of State Incentives for Renewables and Efficiency (www.dsireusa.org) is one place to start.

Insulation

Use the highest R-value insulation you can afford at the time of building. Insulate walls, roofs or attics, foundations, and any opening: wall switches, outlets, window and door frames, and so on. A house wrap applied over the wall sheathing during construction will keep the wind out and is also a good moisture barrier to protect against dampness.

In a colder climate, I would consider windows with a high R factor. You might also consider storm windows to place over thermopane windows to conserve even more energy.

Some homeowners have been known to complain that an airtight home doesn't breathe properly and can get stuffy and stale. But an airtight cabin is simply more energy efficient; you can crack a window if you want fresh air.

Be sure to insulate your hot water heater. I find the hot water insulation kits on the market to be too thin. Instead, I usually use the 5½-inch insulation designed for use with 6-inch-thick wall construction. Also insulate hot water pipes. A great deal of heat (and energy) is lost in hot water pipes before the water is delivered to the faucet.

Ceiling Fans

Ceiling fans can do a lot to keep a cabin comfortable. Most ceiling fans operate at several speeds. They also have reverse switches. In the summer, they are a less expensive alternative to air conditioning. In the winter, they can be reversed and run at low speed to draw warm air from ceilings and circulate it down the walls.

Lower Thermostats

If your cabin heat is thermostat controlled, the temperature during the day does not need to be set above 65 degrees. At night it can be lowered to 60 degrees. In fact, with an electric blanket, sleepers can be comfortable in 45-degree temperatures.

A programmable thermostat is a good idea. They can be set to reduce temperatures during the night and return temperatures to normal just before you get out of bed.

I like sleeping in sleeping bags, whether in a tent, trailer, or cabin. I prefer sleeping bags that are canvas on the outside and lined with flannel. I have several: a lightweight summer bag, a 20-degree bag, and an arctic –40-degree bag. In cool weather, I unzip the bags and sleep on one and cover myself with the other. When nights are around 40 degrees I sleep on top of the arctic bag and use the 20-degree bag for a quilt. In very cold weather I reverse the sleeping bags. When sleeping temperatures are near 20 degrees or lower, I use the summer bag as a liner in the arctic bag and zip them both up. With a wool cap on my head I have slept in snow caves comfortably.

Wind-Powered Irrigation

From the mid-1970s to the mid-1980s, I owned a working farm. The water source for the farm was a large spring. I built an underground cistern to capture runoff water leaving the spring. At a local junkyard, I found a wind pump, originally designed to pump water, with its pump mechanism missing. I erected the tower and rotor and installed a truck alternator connected to the rotor with several pulleys (to step up the rpms). I added a solar-electric panel to the system. I connected the alternator and solar panel to several deep cycle batteries through the truck voltage regulator and a control system to keep the batteries from being overcharged. I then coupled this power system with a 12-volt DC water pump and a drip irrigation system from an RV. Although this was a primitive system, it watered my garden nicely for the eight years I owned that farm.

Waterless or Low-Water-Use Toilets

Low-gallons-per-flush (low-GPF) toilets can save water, energy, and septic system use. The new low-GPF toilets on the market today work remarkably better than the designs of 20 years ago.

An even better option would be a waterless toilet, sometimes called a composting toilet. See chapter 6 for more details.

Heating/Cooling System Maintenance

Regular yearly cleaning of all the parts of your heating or cooling system will increase its efficiency and reduce energy use. Keep chimneys, stovepipes, and furnace filters clean. Keep air ducts, radiators, and fans clean and free from blockages. Remember, heat has to circulate to be effective.

Lighting

The fluorescents of today are of a much higher quality than those of even just a few years ago, and they are much more energy efficient than incandescent bulbs. Light-emitting diode (LED) lighting is another excellent option, because of its miserly use of energy and extremely long life. These LEDs are very efficient because they do not produce much heat; nearly 100 percent of the electricity they consume is converted into light energy.

Shade Trees

The best way to reduce cooling costs in the summer is with shade trees. Properly sited, they will block sunlight from falling on your cabin roof. Trees absorb the sun's energy to carry out photosynthesis, converting it into carbohydrates instead of letting it make your cabin hot. In northern climates, deciduous trees are a good choice, as they will shed their leaves in the colder months and allow for solar heating of your cabin.

Avoid Energy Hogs

Always purchase energy-efficient appliances (Energy Star rated, if possible), even the small countertop ones such as toasters, coffee makers, and so on. A few pennies saved on electricity to operate a toaster each month may not seem like much, but over the life of the toaster, it will pay for the toaster. That's like getting a toaster for free!

Clothes dryers are absolute energy hogs. Instead, invest in a clothes drying rack or a clothesline. In summer, you can hang your clothes outdoors on a clothesline. (You can take it down when it's not in use if you want.) In winter, set up your clothes drying rack near your stove or furnace and your clothes will be dry in no time. I like to dry clothing on a clothesline in the cellar until it's almost dry. I then pop the clothes in the dryer with a dryer sheet and they come out in a few minutes dry, wrinkle free, and smelling good.

Air conditioning is one of the largest energy users in the home. Minimizing or eliminating air conditioning is a great way to save energy. Good natural ventilation and insulation will go a long way to eliminate the need for air conditioning. The extra insulation will also save energy in the winter months. Ceiling fans use far less energy than do air conditioners, and they can be run in reverse in the winter to circulate warm air off the ceiling and down the walls. Sleeping porches are a great way to beat the heat without air conditioning. The house I currently live in has a large, enclosed back porch. The windows of the porch allow it to be used comfortably in all but the coldest weather. One of my guilty pleasures is to sleep there on hot August nights. With a sleeping bag on the pullout sofa in the sitting area, I'm happy and comfortable there on the hottest of nights. I awake to the rising sun and the birds at the bird feeder.

GREEN BUILDING

Green building is the new mantra of architecture. And cabin designers and builders who are interested in off-the-grid power systems are also usually interested in green building. Green building is based on several principles:

➳ **Low environmental impact:** building in concert with nature, not in opposition to nature

➳ **Energy efficiency:** well-insulated and low energy consuming buildings

➳ **Use of sustainable resources and materials:** using renewable materials wherever possible; avoiding potentially dangerous materials such as formaldehyde or ozone-depleting materials

➳ **Use of salvaged or recycled materials:** reusing materials to make the most of the energy and resources that went into producing them

➳ **Long-range planning for the good of the planet:** habitat for people, including low-maintenance plants and landscaping, and consideration for water drainage from altered landscape areas (such as limiting paving of surface areas, which doesn't allow water to percolate into the ground)

➻ **Cost and financial benefits of going green:** using materials that need little or no maintenance and have a long use life

➻ **Design innovation:** realizing that a structure's function is important; small is better than big

➻ **Flexible and recyclable buildings:** buildings that evolve with changing needs; all materials that go into them should be able to be used again or recycled

➻ **Local economies:** buying locally produced products wherever possible, both to stimulate local economies and to minimize the cost and resource depletion of transportation

OFF-THE-GRID MICRO CABIN

This small cabin's ceiling height is 12 feet, which makes it feel much larger than it is. It also features an outside sink and shower, perfect for showering and dish washing in warm climates. The cabin's dimensions allow it to be constructed off-site and trailered to the building site.

Features
136 square feet
Half kitchen
Half bath
Sleeps 2
Relies on RV components
Can be built off-site and trailered in
Designed to be off the grid

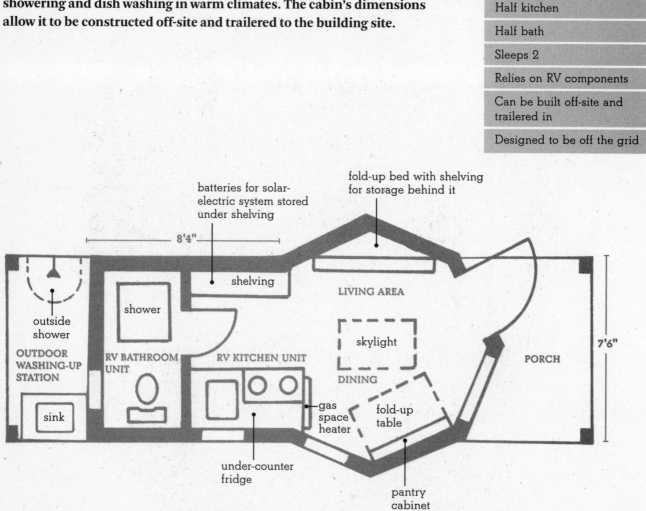

batteries for solar-electric system stored under shelving

fold-up bed with shelving for storage behind it

8'4"

shelving

LIVING AREA

outside shower

shower

skylight

7'6"

OUTDOOR WASHING-UP STATION

RV BATHROOM UNIT

RV KITCHEN UNIT

DINING

PORCH

sink

gas space heater

fold-up table

under-counter fridge

pantry cabinet

OPEN TRUSSES: create 12-foot ceilings, giving the cabin a much larger feel.

SOLAR-ELECTRIC PANELS: allow cabin to be used in areas where traditional electrical service is not available.

OPERABLE SKYLIGHT: brings light to the interior and can be opened for ventilation in warm weather.

solar hot water panels

OUTDOOR SHOWER AND WASH SINK: can be built onto the end of the cabin, with lattice as a privacy screen.

OFF-THE-GRID SHIPPING CONTAINER CABIN

Like the plans featured in chapter 4, this design makes use of a shipping container as its base, with a frame added on. In this case the frame comprises a porch and outdoor washing-up space, which together make the cabin ideal accommodations for warm weather.

Features
160 square feet
Half kitchen
Half bath
Sleeps 2
Relies on RV components
Utilizes one 20-foot shipping container
Designed to be off the grid

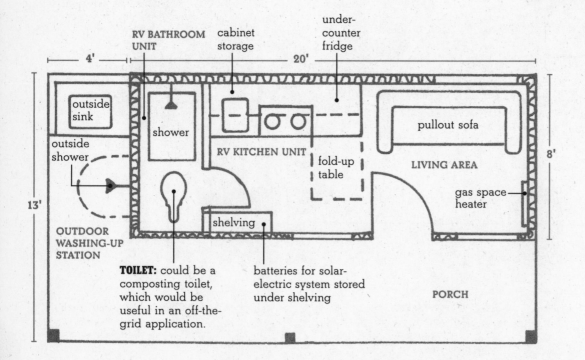

RV BATHROOM UNIT

cabinet storage

under-counter fridge

4'

20'

outside sink

outside shower

shower

RV KITCHEN UNIT

fold-up table

pullout sofa

LIVING AREA

8'

gas space heater

13'

OUTDOOR WASHING-UP STATION

shelving

TOILET: could be a composting toilet, which would be useful in an off-the-grid application.

batteries for solar-electric system stored under shelving

PORCH

= shipping container

storage area above
shipping container

solar
hot water
panel

solar-
electric
panels

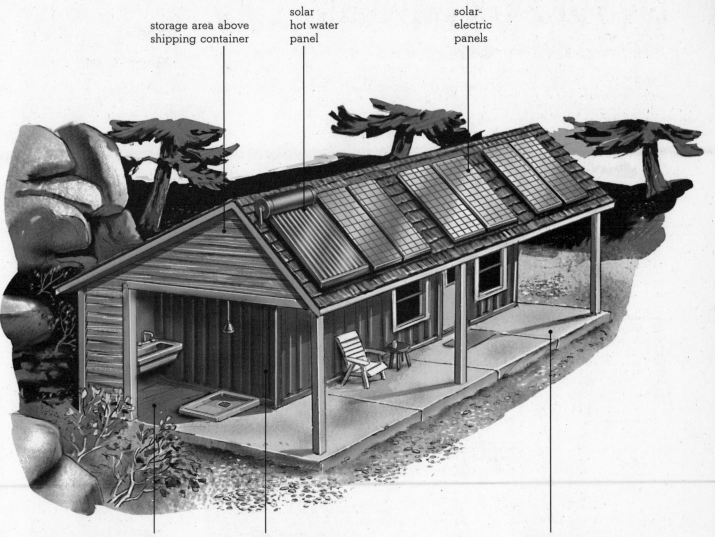

OUTDOOR WASHING-UP AREA:
is great for washing dishes
and showering in warm
weather.

SHIPPING CONTAINER: forms
the base unit of this cabin,
with outdoor living spaces
built around it.

PORCH: is designed with a
deep overhang to provide
plenty of shade.

OFF-THE-GRID EMERSON CABIN

The first floor of this cabin is only 144 square feet. It may not seem like much, but Henry David Thoreau lived and worked for two years, two months, and two days in a 150-foot-square cabin on the property of his friend Ralph Waldo Emerson. If he can do it, so can you.

Features

240 square feet

Half kitchen

Half bath

Sleeps 2 to 4

Relies on RV components

Designed to be off the grid

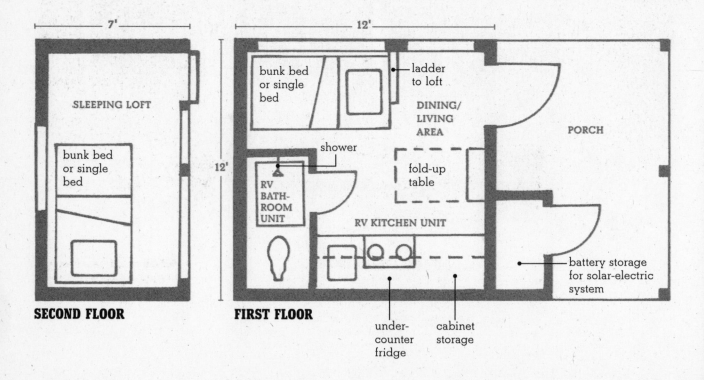

LOFT: in a cabin designed to be used by just one person, could be converted to a retreat space, with a desk for writing, chair for reading, or other accommodations.

WINDOWS: at the peak of the roof bring light to the interior.

solar-electric panels

OUTDOOR STORAGE LOCKER: in an off-the-grid system, provides space for the batteries and control components.

PORCH: could be screened to keep out bugs or framed in as additional living space.

OFF-THE-GRID PASSIVE SOLAR CABIN A

This cabin is only 322 square feet, but the loft ceiling height makes it feel much larger. The passive solar feature is a large glass window opening into the living space. Space heating is provided by a wood-burning stove.

Features
460 square feet
Full kitchen
Three-quarter bath
Sleeps 2 to 4
Relies on RV components
Designed for passive solar heating
Designed to be off the grid

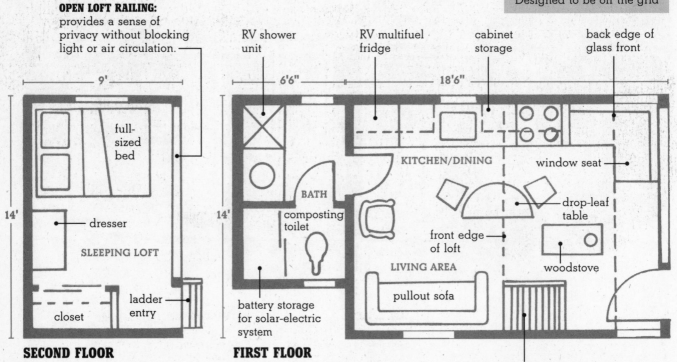

OPEN LOFT RAILING: provides a sense of privacy without blocking light or air circulation.

RV shower unit

RV multifuel fridge

cabinet storage

back edge of glass front

9'

full-sized bed

14'

dresser

SLEEPING LOFT

closet

ladder entry

SECOND FLOOR

6'6"

18'6"

9'

BATH

composting toilet

KITCHEN/DINING

window seat

drop-leaf table

front edge of loft

woodstove

LIVING AREA

14'

battery storage for solar-electric system

pullout sofa

FIRST FLOOR

SHIP'S LADDER: provides storage space underneath for coats and outdoor equipment.

SLEEPING LOFT: is set at the rear of the cabin, leaving the front of the cabin open from floor to roof.

ROOF VENT AND SKYLIGHT: provide natural cooling, allowing rising warm air to escape the interior.

UPPER-LEVEL FRONT WINDOWS: bring light to the loft and allow for natural ventilation.

SOLAR-ELECTRIC PANELS: are set up as a freestanding unit near the cabin; they allow it to be used in areas where traditional electrical service is not available.

GLASS FRONT: works as a passive solar component; a heat sink situated just inside, such as a masonry floor, would improve its heat-absorption capacity.

WINDOW SEAT: is situated at the front of the glass wall, offering unobstructed views to the outside.

OFF-THE-GRID PASSIVE SOLAR CABIN B

This cabin has the same floorprint and passive solar design as the preceding plan, but with a different interior layout. The point is that any cabin design can be changed to accommodate the different needs of different sites and the preferences of the owner.

Features
460 square feet
Full kitchen
Three-quarter bath
Sleeps 2 to 4
Relies on RV components
Designed for passive solar heating
Designed to be off the grid

OPEN LOFT RAILING: provides a sense of privacy without blocking light or air circulation.

SHIP'S LADDER: provides storage space underneath for coats and outdoor equipment.

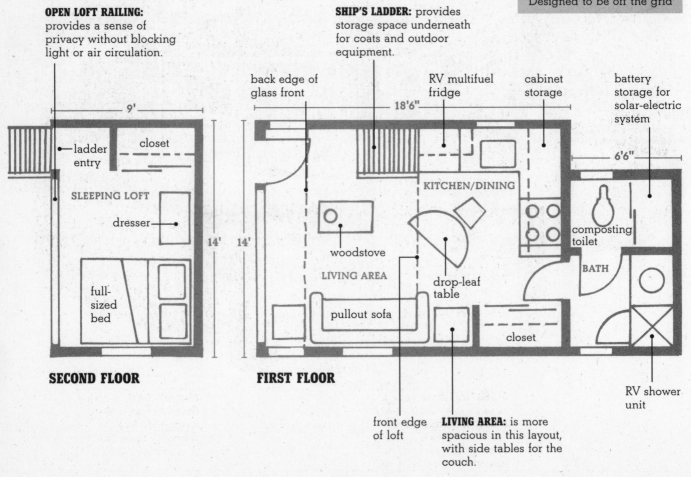

LIVING AREA: is more spacious in this layout, with side tables for the couch.

SOLAR-ELECTRIC PANELS: are set up as a freestanding unit near the cabin; they allow it to be used in areas where traditional electrical service is not available.

ROOF VENT/SKYLIGHT: provides natural cooling, allowing rising warm air to escape the interior.

GLASS FRONT: works as a passive solar component; a heat sink situated just inside, such as a masonry floor, would improve its heat-absorption capacity.

SLEEPING LOFT: is set at the rear of the cabin, leaving the front of the cabin open from floor to roof.

ALPHABETICAL LISTING OF PLANS

INDEX

Page numbers in *italics* indicate illustrations.